Front cover:
Notre-Dame de Paris
Pages 2/3:
Map of Paris and the Exhibition Palace
Pages 6/7
The south façade of Notre-Dame
Page 10:
Mona Lisa
Back cover:
Montmartre

© MOLIÈRE 2002, Paris
ISBN :2.907670.37.9
ISSN : 1158-4386
Printed and bound in Italy

Photographic credits:

Eric Deffontaine: 18a, 28, 29, 34, 38, 39b, 64, 66, 74, 84, 102/103, 105.
Hirou/Yargui: 19.
Eparzier: 1, 6/7, 13, 14, 15, 17, 18b, 20, 21, 23, 24/25, 27, 30, 31, 33, 35b, 36, 37, 39a, 40, 43, 45, 46, 48, 52, 53, 55, 59, 60, 63, 67, 68/69, 70, 75, 76/77, 78, 79, 80, 81, 83, 85, 88, 89, 90, 91, 92/93, 95, 96, 97, 98, 99, 104, 106, 107, 108, 109, 129, 136.
Hirou/Yargui: 19.
Pix: 51, 57, 73, 86, 101.
Wawczak: 131.

Collaboration : F.B.S.B.

A CELEBRATION OF
PARIS

Foreword
Jacques Chirac

MOLIÈRE

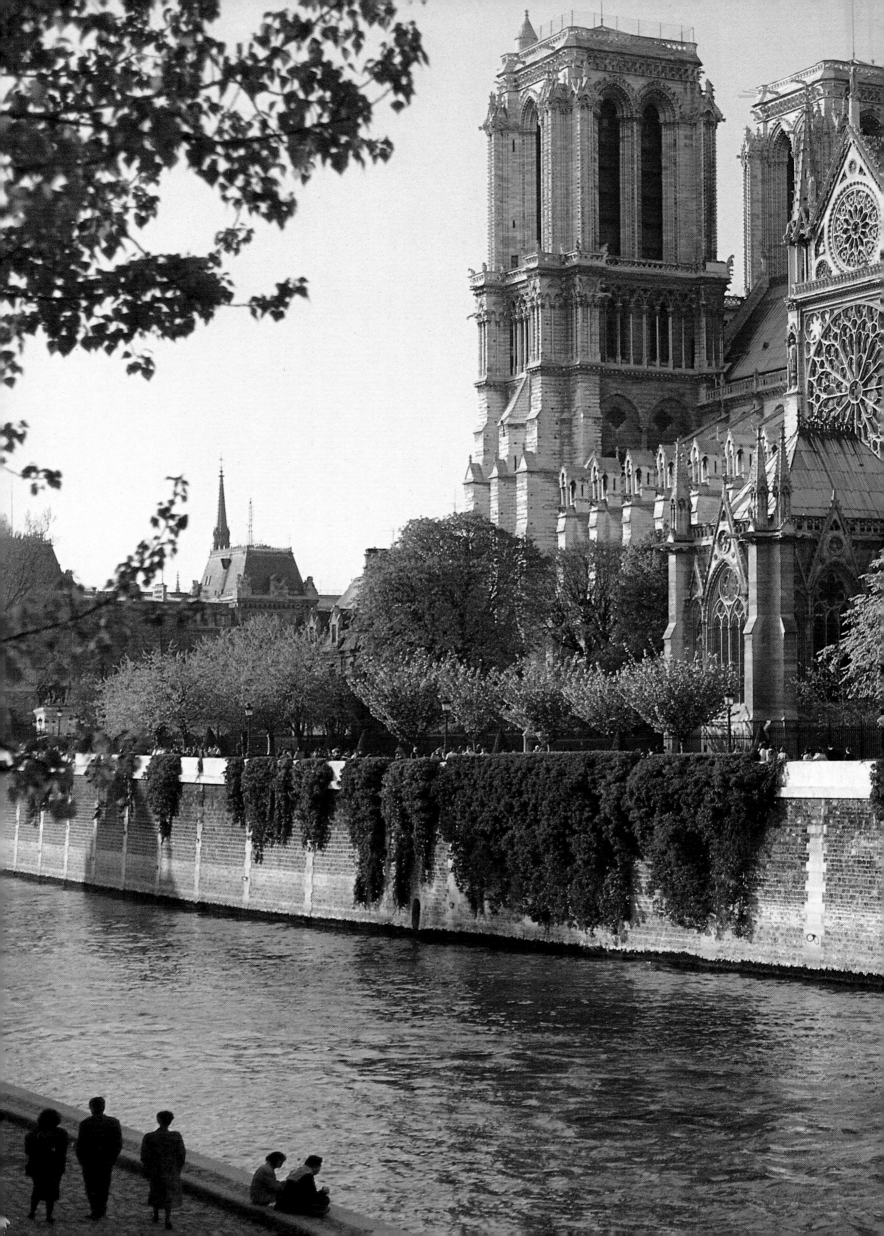

A CELEBRATION OF
PARIS

The Mayor of Paris

FOREWORD

For centuries, Paris has been the privileged meeting place of philosophers and artists from the four corners of the globe. By welcoming effrontery, and hence fostering creativity, it has become a unique center of culture, described at several moments in its history – and rightfully so – as the "new Athens," where ideas are freely expressed and debated, and the arts flourish in their full diversity.

The treasures, monuments, streets and promenades have all been profoundly marked by the city's intense intellectual and artistic effervescence, and at the same time, they testify to the history of France in which Paris, as the capital, has played a pre-eminent role. It is fitting that a new book on Paris should be added to the prestigious collection devoted to the most outstanding works produced by human genius.

Sometimes scorned, but more often adored, Paris is the monster and marvel that inspired Montaigne to make one of his most tender declarations of affection: "I love Paris," he confided, "warts and all (... and) if I am French, it is only through this great city – great in its people, great in its nobility, and above all, great and incomparable in its diversity and variety; (...) it is the glory of France and one of the world's most noble ornaments."

The face of the French capital has, of course, changed a great deal since Montaigne first described it, and it has been continually enriched with new monuments and building projects, including the Georges Pompidou Center, the Forum des Halles, the Bercy Sports Palace, the Institute of the Arab World and the Louvre Pyramid. All these additions have, in turn, contributed to the enchantment of visitors, shared long ago by George Sand. "I know of no other city," she wrote, "where strollers can enjoy more pleasant daydreams." Today, beyond its transformations and legitimate aspirations to be a modern capital, Paris still touches and delights those who explore it on foot.

A celebration of Paris is an irresistible invitation to wander through the streets of Paris, get a sense of the Capital, dream about the centuries gone by and cross paths with the intangible yet ever-present shadows of famous statesmen, writers and artists from all over the world who have made it the "City of Light."

Jacques CHIRAC

CONTENTS

THE ISLANDS

Île de la Cité

With its admirable location in the geographical heart of Paris, the Île de la Cité possesses a unique cultural and historical heritage. From an architectural standpoint, the island alone would justify a stay in Paris, if only because of Notre-Dame and Sainte-Chapelle. For atmosphere, Place Dauphine, the flower market and even, in a completely different vein, Quai des Orfèvres, are all worth a visit. The island has no close competitors for points of interest, if one adds the Conciergerie, the Hôtel-Dieu, the tiny old Rue Chanoinesse and the Vert-Galant and Notre-Dame squares. Here, on this magnificent island, every stone seems to have a story to tell. Even the ground itself is the result of both the passage of time and the work of man, for in bygone days, the island measured only 25 acres, not 42 as it does today, and it was level with the Seine.

At the outset, nothing could have foretold the island's brilliant future. At a time when cities in the Orient had been renowned for hundreds or even thousands of years for their intellectual and artistic development, the future Gaul was nothing but wastelands. In Hallstadt, Austria, the civilization of the Celts, probably from the eastern steppes, came into prominence. These people were organised into tribes, one of which, the Parisii, settled on the marshy land, rich in waterfowl and fish, located between the two branches of the Seine.

The French capital had taken shape or, at least, had come into existence. There were decisive factors prompting the decision to settle here: it was easy to access the island from the southern bank (what would later be called the Left Bank) since the Seine was calm in that area. Soon, two bridges were put up, allowing settlers quick access to the mainland. However, the island's rural vocation was not to last long, for the Romans were swiftly progressing.

They seized the island in the year 52 B.C., but had little interest in its limited activities of fishing and hunting. Their colonisation was mainly architectural: they were master-builders. Here was an island, located on a perfect site, where everything was still to be done. Notre-Dame and the Palace of Justice are currently located on the site where the Romans had built the palace of the prefect and a temple dedicated to Jupiter. Nearby, they also erected an altar to worship the goddess Isis whom the Romans had taken from the Egyptian pantheon. Roman public life took place between these two large constructions, on the vast forum esplanade.

The Cité was a prosperous area, and trade was organised and governed by the powerful corporation of the Nautes (Roman river boatmen). However, the island was too small to accommodate everyone, and people began living on the Left Bank. The situation changed at the end of the 3rd century, when the Barbarians invaded. The inhabitants fled to the island and built a surrounding wall to protect themselves. Two centuries later, the Francs, another Barbarian tribe, did not spare Paris. Clovis, their chief, made the city his capital, putting an end to any further Roman influence. The population overflowed once again, and when the Normans invaded, the inhabitants of Paris again took refuge on the island. Roman colonisation had made the island the center of religious and political power. It was populated, depopulated and repopulated again with each new invasion, but it was not until the second millennium that the face of the Cité began to change. The island took on a new dimension in 1163 when the canon Maurice de Sully decided to build a seat of religious authority worthy of the French capital. Abbot Suger had built a splendid cathedral in Saint-Denis, and the Bishop of Paris wanted an equally prestigious construction.

The south façade of Notre-Dame

When coming upon the lacy stone that has succeeded in resisting the passage of time, one can only admire the builders of the cathedral. The faith of the compagnons or master-builders was so strong that they communicated their enthusiasm to the entire population of Paris. It became a joyful hive of activity, and everyone made it a point of honor to participate. The flow of people generated countless small jobs, but there were also many volunteers, such as the women who met regularly to prepare food for the workers and serve it on the cathedral square.

Page 14:
The towers

For centuries, the two towers that stand 227 feet above the ground, have come to be a symbol of unchanging Paris. more than the cathedral's 295-foot spire erected by Viollet-le-Duc.

Notre-Dame de Paris

The cathedral stands in the heart of Paris, marking the zero-kilometer point from which the distance to all the cities of France is calculated, and the network of roadways and highways branches out.

The first Christian settlers had transformed that Roman temple dedicated to Jupiter into a basilica, and at the beginning of the 4th century, the King of Paris, Childebert, ordered the reconstruction of the building. The new church was dedicated to the martyr Saint Etienne and a church dedicated to Mary was joined to it. The building was burned down by the Normans, and was then rebuilt as a Romanesque church during the 9th century and embellished thereafter.

In the 12th century, the site was chosen by the Bishop of Paris, Maurice de Sully, who obtained the necessary authorisation from the church authorities and from the king himself, and set about building Notre-Dame Cathedral. The Middle Ages was the time of guilds, each of which developed rigorous rules linked to a distinct form of solidarity.

The *compagnons* or "fellows" of the various guilds respected each other, and joined together with great enthusiasm on the construction of this monument. The cathedral is considered a masterpiece of Gothic style architecture, although it still presents some traces of the Romanesque style.

The construction went on for eighty years, during the reigns of three monarchs: Louis VII, Philippe Auguste and Saint-Louis, but it took another century for it to become the magnificent cathedral visitors see today.

At the beginning of the 14th century, Notre-Dame, standing at the centre of the island, was a source of incomparable prestige.

The cathedral stood on the same square, which was much smaller than it is today.

In the 17th century, the high altar and the rood screen were reconstructed, and enhanced with marble and bronze decorations. During the 18th century, Soufflot tore down the central pier and tympanum to make more room for the royal canopy during processions. At the time of the Revolution, the *sans-culottes* knocked over the twenty-eight statues representing the Kings of Judea and Israel (the ancestors of Christ).

The publication of Victor Hugo's novel, *Notre-Dame de Paris* in 1831, contributed to the opinion that the cathedral should be restored.

Viollet-le-Duc carried out the works between 1845 and 1864. In the centre, the great portal represents the scene of the Last Judgement. It is dominated by the statue of Christ, who is separating the chosen from the damned, while the latter wait to be saved through the intercession of the Virgin Mary or Saint John who appear, kneeling, on either side of the supreme judge. This is the tallest and widest portal, but in the cannon of Gothic aesthetics, symmetry was by no means required.

The east end of the cathedral

The stunning flying buttresses that rest upon the east end of the cathedral have often been said to resemble the sails of a ship. The garden and neo-Gothic fountain were built in 1844 on the site of the archdiocese and the chapels, which were demolished in the 19th century along with all the other buildingss surrounding the cathedral at the time of its construction.

Variety was encouraged, and hence the portal of the Virgin on the left is taller than the one dedicated to St. Anne on the right.

A large, delicately designed rose window (33 feet in diameter) illuminates the center of the façade. Small patches of sky can be seen through the arches of the large gallery with its tall, slender columns, producing a feeling of lightness with its lace of stone. It is surmounted by a balustrade decorated with imps, strange birds and monsters typical of Gothic iconography.

The towers with their four long windows, 52 feet high, give the construction such a sense of harmony that the builders felt they did not need to add spires.

Visitors should definitely climb up the 387 stairs leading to a spectacular view of the city center, where one can admire the marvellous sixteen-ton tenor bell while searching for the shadow of Quasimodo.

No visitor should leave without walking around Notre-Dame, from the southern portal of St. Etienne to the portal of the Cloister, with its magnificent rose windows and a crown of flying buttresses that make the east end of the church looks like the prow of a ship. Viollet-le-Duc added a long spire to the whole, which rises up 295 feet towards the sky. The cathedral itself is 426 feet long, 164 feet wide and 115 high; it can seat 9,000 people. Parts of the rose windows on the façade and the transept are still the original 13th century stained glass, although most of them were reconstructed during the 1960s.

Thus, the Christians erected the first buildings of the capital on the site of the monument to the Nautes, the notables of Lutetia, to whom the city owes its coat of arms. Since then, countless abbeys, churches and outbuildings have been added, but it was Notre-Dame in Paris that gave France worldwide authority in religious matters, and still attracts thousands of visitors every year, a proof of its international reputation.

Notre-Dame is still a Parisian house of worship, with its own stories and current religious activities. One of the most famous anecdotes refers to the wedding of Henri IV and Margaret of Valois, which was celebrated without the King being present, because he had not yet converted and was still a Protestant! The most famous 20th century story concerns the conversion of Paul Claudel, who received the Christian faith while standing beside a pillar inside the cathedral, where an engraved flagstone recalls the event.

The Hôtel-Dieu Hospital is located in the cathedral square. In former times, there was a hospital bearing the same name on the other side of the square, which was the only building that stood out over the Seine.

Sainte-Chapelle

Saint-Louis (Louis the Blessed) bought the Crown of Thorns and other relics from the Latin emperor Baldwin of Constantinople.

To have a place to keep these precious and expensive relics, Louis IX ordered the construction of Sainte-Chapelle in a record time of only three years. In 1248, Parisians were astounded by the sight of this jewel of Gothic art, and in the 21st century visitors are still fascinated by the same windows bearing 1,134 biblical scenes on over 6,650 square feet of glass, displaying exceptional precision and brilliance.

The arches rest on thin pillars, and simple reinforcement has balanced the construction perfectly, without a single flying buttress. The stained-glass windows rise to a height of 50 feet, and the spire reaches 246 feet. The construction has suffered many fires, and was last restored in 1854. The façade is framed by two towers with long spires, and is preceded by a double portico surmounted by a loggia and a delicate rose window that was reconstructed during the 15th century.

Inside there are two superimposed chapels, in the style of other palatine chapels. The lower chapel is reminiscent of a crypt as it is just 23 feet high and 55 wide. The central nave is flanked by two small naves with light flying buttresses. The pillar columns are slender and elegant.

This chapel was once used by servants and palace guards and is not very well-lit. The stained-glass windows have been restored, and it is richly decorated with gold on red or blue backgrounds. Flagstones are inscribed with the names of the canons who are buried in the chapel.

Two spiral staircases lead to the upper chapel, where twelve windows illuminate the stained-glass nave. Each of the twelve pillars is decorated with one of the apostles carrying a cross.

The upper chapel was designed to hold the Sacred Relics, and is decorated with sculptures that look like

Sainte-Chapelle

Often considered the jewel of Gothic art, the splendor of this church is due to restoration carried out by Viollet-le-Duc, Lassus and Duban, following Pierre de Montereau's plans, although the steeple dates from the 15th century. Sainte-Chapelle is located on the grounds of the Palace of Justice, built against the Conciergerie, which is where visitors enter.

Pont-Neuf

The oldest bridge in Paris was an innovative construction. It was the first of its kind built without any houses and the first to introduce the notion of sidewalks in the capital. Many small shops were installed under its arches, making it a lively spot from which Parisians could contemplate the flow of the Seine for the first time. At the west end, there is a charming garden, known as the Vert-Galant, which is a river-level replica of the triangular geometry of Place Dauphine.

carved ivory. The reliquary is located at the top of the gallery, although the Crown of Thorns was taken to Notre-Dame.

From left to right, one can read the whole Bible in the stained-glass windows. The story of the creation of Sainte-Chapelle is also shown in the windows, and one can read how Baldwin sold Christ's Crown of Thorns to Venetian pawnbrokers to defend his empire against the Saracens. As he could not settle his debt, he proposed that Louis IX pay off the Venetians and keep the Crown.

Pierre de Montereau – also known as Pierre de Montreuil – has been credited with the construction of Sainte-Chapelle, although there is no documentary evidence for this theory.

The Conciergerie

Charles V abandoned this construction in favor of the Louvre and the Hotel Saint-Paul, and the palace kept the name of the only part of it that came under the authority of the king's *concierge*, a sort of superintendent in charge of the building.

The beautiful façade reminds us that this building was once a prestigious palace used by Philippe the Fair and his successors as their residence, before it was turned into a prison.

On one of the corners, the square tower is decorated with the first large clock installed in Paris, ordered by Charles V in 1371 and made by Henri de Vic. It was rebuilt in 1583 by Germain Pilon during the reign

of Henri III, and was decorated with the ornaments still visible today: a coat of arms and a floral decoration, with the figures of Justice and the Law on either side. Another floor and a belfry were built on top of it in 1848.

In the center, there are twin towers named the Tour de César and the Tour d'Argent, which frame the original entrance to the palace. The last tower is the Tour Bonbec, the only castellated element on the building.

One enters the building by the Guard Hall with a vaulted ceiling supported by sturdy pillars.

The Hall of the Men-at-Arms is one of the most beautiful Gothic-style halls, along with those at Mont-Saint-Michel and the Palace of the Popes in Avignon.

Under the Old Regime, the building was used for the internment of political prisoners, such as Montgomery who mortally wounded King Henri II in a tournament and Ravillac who assassinated Henri IV and famous bandits such as Cartouche and Mandrin.

The Revolutionary Tribunal imprisoned many famous personalities such as Marie-Antoinette and Madame Elisabeth (sister of Louis XVI), Madame Roland and Charlotte Corday, Lavoisier and André Chénier, Hébert and Cloots, Danton and Camille Desmoulins, Robespierre, Saint-Just and finally the public prosecutor himself, Fouquier-Tinville.

Pont-Neuf

Although its name means "New Bridge", Pont-Neuf is actually the oldest bridge in Paris, as well as the most beautiful and most famous. It was painted by Turner and wrapped by Christo in 1985.

The Cité already had four bridges during the Middle Ages, but they were very crowded and ferryboats only crossed the Seine during the day. Henri III decided to build a fifth bridge in 1577.

Construction work was halted during the civil war, and finally Henri IV decided to build a bridge without houses on either side, incorporating sidewalks for pedestrians. The bridge was inaugurated in 1604 and became a favorite spot for promenades for the idle rich as well as merchants, charlatans and pickpockets.

The *bouquinistes* or the secondhand booksellers set their trade up here and started to compete with bookshops.

A statue of Henri IV was erected in 1614, four years after his assassination. It was the first royal statue in Paris to be exhibited outdoors, and also the first equestrian statue of its kind. The Revolutionaries melted the statue down, and placed a new one representing the Tables of the Rights of Mankind on the pedestal. The statue that is currently located on the bridge was not created until 1818.

The Palace of Justice

The first building erected on this site was a palace for a Roman governor, followed by an imperial palace in the year 360. Clovis and the early Merovingians lived in the building, although their successors decided to set up their residences in other cities, and left Paris to be governed by its bishops and then counts who settled in the palace. The Normans seized the palace on three occasions (in 845, 856 and 861) when they took the rest of the Cité, but they were driven back after the seige of 885-886. Saint-Louis erected a new palace here in the 13th century, which was enlarged by Philip the Fair in the 14th century, and was stormed in 1358 by rebellious

The Clock

Parisians have been able to tell the time on this clock since 1371. It was the city's first public clock, redesigned by Germain Pilon, Catherine de Medicis' favourite sculptor. It bears an inscription recalling that Henri III was crowned King of Poland in 1573, before succeeding his brother Charles IX the following year.

(Opposite page)
The Conciergerie

During the 18th century, this part of the ancient palace used by the Capetian kings was used as a prison for those sent to the guillotine by the revolutionaries, including Marie-Antoinette. Its Gothic-style halls, especially the Hall of the Men-at-Arms, are among of the most beautiful examples of their kind.

Place Dauphine

Place Dauphine

This square dates from the childhood of Louis XIII, when Harlay, the president of the Parliament, bought the land from Henri IV and developed it. It was named Place Dauphine in honour of young Prince Louis. From here, one can contemplate the west entrance to the Palace of Justice, usually assimilated with its nord façade, Quai des Orfèvre. The word "orfèvre" means "goldsmith", referring to the jewellers who once did business in this area.

Opposite page:
**A façade
in Place Dauphine**

Though they have been repeatedly restored, some of the red brick and stone façades still look the same as they did centuries ago.

merchants led by the provost Etienne Marcel. The advisers of the dauphin Charles were killed here before his eyes, and later, when he became Charles V, he abandoned the palace and its bloody memories, preferring to use the Louvre or Hôtel Saint-Paul as his royal residence.

The building became the seat of the Parisian Parliament. It was the city's Supreme Court of Justice, and its magistrates were appointed by the king. In 1522, Francis I sold the parliamentary seats, which became hereditary from then on.

The members of Parliament grew more independent and set off the revolts of the Fronde (1648-1653). Louis XIV managed to subdue them, but it was Louis XV who finally put an end to them in 1771. Louis XVI reintroduced Parliament once again, but not for long, as the Constituent Assembly dissolved it in 1789.

The revolutionary tribunals took over the building and the Palace of Parliament became the Palace of Justice. The large iron gate dates from the reign of Louis XVI (1785). The building was reconstructed in 1776, after a fire.

Place Dauphine

This used to be the king's orchard, and in 1607, Henri IV ordered the area to be surveyed and put Achille Harlay, the first president of the Parliament, in charge of construction.

Houses were built on all three sides of the triangular square, following the same model: a ground floor with broadstone arcades, two floors with brick and stone façades, covered by a slate roof decorated with skylights.

It was named Dauphine to honor the young dauphin, who was only six years old at the time it was constructed but would become Louis XIII three years later.

The south side was torn down in 1874 to reveal the extremely elaborate façade of the Palace of Justice. There are only a few original façades left. In spite of these mutilations, the square is still a charming spot, offering a "provincial" feeling in the very center of the capital.

Île Saint-Louis

The quays and streets of Île Saint-Louis have been spared the hustle and bustle of the metro and shopping areas, and the island is one of the most pleasant places to walk, especially for lovers.

Henri IV had planned to make it an extension of the nearby Marais, but due to his premature death, the construction of the new quarter was not carried out until the reign of Louis XIII. The buildings were laid out evenly, in keeping with the style of the period, adding an atmosphere of quiet harmony to the charming 17th century façades.

Baudelaire, who lived on the Quai d'Anjou, may have found the inspiration for his verses in this spot: "Here, everything is order and beauty, luxury, quiet and delight."

The island only came to be known as Saint-Louis in the 18th century. Until 1614, it belonged to the chapter of Notre-Dame, and was divided into two small islands. The first of these was known as Notre-Dame Island and the second as Cow Island (east of Rue Poulletier). In those days, there was nothing luxurious about the area; it was simply a rural domain.

Between 1620 and 1650, the pastures were used for the construction of large mansions built by Louis and Francis Le Vau, with finely-wrought gates and façades adorned with masks, balconies and wrought-iron, and behind them, paved courtyards that have not changed since their creation.

According to legend, Restif de La Bretonne enjoyed inscribing a record of his amorous adventures on the stone walls during his stays on the island. On the day his wife left him, he carved the phrase: "Today, the monster is gone."

Although none of his graffiti remains, one should still walk around the area, as in the Marais, looking up to appreciate the details of the narrow streets. The quays and bridges offer wonderful views of the east end of Notre-Dame and the church of Saint-Gervais.

This tiny island, which has lost none of its charm, has been solidly linked to both banks of the river since the 17th century. As with most bridges in Paris, the houses along the island bridges disappeared and were rebuilt later on.

Pont Louis-Philippe extends to the right bank, forming a counterpart to Pont Saint-Louis, which joins the island to the Ile de la Cité and has a charm all its own as the only footbridge. There is also Pont Marie, named after the businessman who completed its construction in 1635, and Pont Sully, built in 1876, which is located to the east, and bears the same name on both sides of the river.

Pont de la Tournelle was the first to join the island to the Left Bank, and was built at the beginning of the 16th century. The first construction was made of wood and had to be rebuilt a number of times after fires and deterioration. The current bridge dates from the beginning of the 20th century. During the 17th century, there was a well on the bridge, where water carriers were supplied.

On the site of what used to be the Saint-Bernard Gate in the walls built by Philippe Auguste, a tall statue of Sainte Geneviève watches over the Seine. Her prayers are believed to have saved the inhabitants of Lutetia from Attila's armies.

One of the first constructions on the Ile Saint-Louis was a church located midway along a road running the length of the island: Rue Saint-Louis-en-Île. The building was enlarged in 1634, when it became a parish church. The works were delayed, however, due to the death of Le Vau, and the church was not consecrated until 1725.

Large residences were finally completed during this era, and most of them were occupied by famous artists or aristocrats.

In the 19th century, Count Zamoiski founded a Polish library in the mansion located to the south, on the Quai d'Orléans, which onced belonged to one of the king's secretaries and is now owned by the Polish Academy of Science and Arts. From 1729 onwards, no. 16 Quai de Béthune became the residence of Maréchal de Richelieu, as successful on the battlefields as he was in his amorous escapades.

Other beautiful vestiges are found on the north side of the island, on the Quai de Bourbon and especially the Quai d'Anjou, where the Hôtel de Lauzun and the Hôtel de Lambert, both built by Le Vau, are located.

The Comte de Lauzun, a highly colorful character, was imprisoned by Louis XIV for ten years in the Pignerol Fortress, as the latter opposed his marriage to the King's first cousin, the Duchess de Montpensier (known as "La Grande Mademoiselle"). He nonetheless managed to marry her in secret.

The mansion next belonged to the Marquis de Richelieu, the cardinal's great-nephew, who gave sumptuous parties with his wife, and then to the Marquis de Pimodan. Charles Baudelaire lived here for a while and devoted himself to "artificial paradises" as a member of the *Club des Haschichins*, together with Théophile Gautier (his neighbor), Alexandre Dumas and Eugène Delacroix.

Since 1928, the City of Paris has used the building to hold large receptions, where guests are given a taste of the 17th century through the décor by Lepautre, Le Brun or Patel.

The entrance to the Hôtel de Lambert is located on Rue Saint-Louis-en-l'Île, and the construction was also decorated by artists who worked at Versailles: Le Sueur and Le Brun. The building has a "Love Cabinet" and a Gallery of Hercules, imitating the ones at Versailles. Following the trend created by Le Vau and the architects of his time, the rich, sumptuous interiors are concealed behind simple, austere façades, softened on the north side by beautifully preserved gardens.

The mansion was built for Lambert de Thorigny, the president of the Chamber of Appeals of the Parisian Parliament, and was embellished by his son, who made it into a remarkably elegant complex.

After belonging to various owners, in the early 18th century, the building came to be owned by the Marquise de Châtelet, who was close to Voltaire for many years. He was her guest there for some time in 1742. In the 19th century, the building, like its neighbor, was bought by a Polish family, the Czartoryskis. The new family maintained the building's artistic tradition, and Delacroix, Chopin and George Sand were among its illustrious visitors.

Hôtel de Lambert

This mansion, the most beautiful hôtel particulier of the 17th-century, benefited greatly from Fouquet's wise choice of architects to whom the Sun King later entrusted the building of Versailles. On the outside, it presents rounded broadstone façades that come to life in the sunlight, and on the inside, a magnificent gallery dedicated to Hercules, with the same name and splendor as the one in Versailles.

Next pages:
The quays

The charm of the island lies in the sumptuous hôtels particuliers along the banks and the quays that have remained unchanged since the era when Daubigny, Daumier, Baudelaire and Théophile Gautier decided to move here.

THE LEFT BANK

The Latin Quarter

Saint-Michel Fountain

Thousands of students from all over the world use the familiar silhouette of Saint Michael slaying the dragon as a meeting point. The fountain is a relatively modern construction compared to others in the Latin Quarter. It was designed by Davioud, an architect who frequently worked with Haussmann.

Page 28:
Cluny Museum

The Romans passed on their art of living, especially their use of public baths, to the Gauls. During the 3rd century, they built vast thermal baths and gardens extending all the way to the Seine. However, at the end of that century, the Barbarians sacked the area. After ten and a half centuries, the Abbey of Cluny bought the land to house abbots during their stays in Paris. Between 1485 and 1500, the Bishop of Clermont rebuilt the residence we see today. The splendid late-Gothic-style construction has accommodated famous guests such as Mary of England, the widow of Louis XII, and Mazarin visited as Papal Nuncio. At the time of the Revolution, the property was confiscated and sold. The building went through a number of owners until Alexandre du Sommerard bought it for his collection of art works in 1833. Nowadays, Cluny displays the treasures of medieval France, including the Lady and the Unicorn *tapestries which are the jewel of the collection. The ruins of the thermal baths are still visible beneath it.*

This area owes its name to the fact that, until the Revolution, Latin was the official language used in the university, and not to Roman vestiges, as some people think. In fact, Paris is one of the cities that preserved the fewest traces of the Roman conquest. The quarter has been a university center ever since Abélard took refuge on Sainte-Geneviève hill, when it acquired the friendly, tumultuous atmosphere of students it has kept to this day.

During the 1950s, the quarter still had a unique aura, even compared to foreign universities. However, the increasing number of students led to the creation of new universities very different from the traditional Sorbonne, where, between the wars, Bergson taught well-bred ladies whose chauffeurs waited at the door wearing frock coats.

Some prestigious establishments resisted being transferred, such as Lycée Louis-le-Grand (once the renowned College de Clermont, a Jesuit institution), Lycée Saint-Louis (once the College d'Harcourt), Lycée Henri IV and the Ecole Normale Supérieure, but even the Ecole Polytechnique has left Sainte-Geneviève hill.

Few students walk along the Boulevard Saint-Michel or the steep streets of La Contrescarpe today devising schemes to change the world, and tourists are sometimes amazed at how commercial the quarter has become, after earning itself a reputation for intellectual effervescence.

Although the area belongs to the 5th arrondissement, no one can agree on its actual limits. Thus, the Latin Quarter includes parts of the 6th arrondissement such as the Luxembourg Gardens and Saint-Germain-des-Prés, the areas around other universities such as the School of Medicine and even the law faculty of Assas. By extension, it also includes the vicinity of Place Maubert.

Saint-Séverin

This quarter, located near the Seine, is one of the oldest in Paris. Its name comes from a 6th century hermit called Séverin, who built a chapel that was burned down by the Normans. It was rebuilt a century later, when it took on importance by drawing all the Parisians living on the Left Bank. In 1198, Pope Innocent III ordered Foulques, the abbot of Neuilly-sur-Marne, to move to this chapel and preach the Fourth Crusade, which led to the storming of Constantinople (1204) and made Baldwin the first Latin Emperor of the Orient. The church was rebuilt and enlarged over the next three centuries. The architect who worked on the building during the 15th century respected the original structure; hence, Saint-Séverin is still a splendid example of flamboyant Gothic style (except for additions made in the 17th century).

The surrounding area, leading to the Seine, consists of small streets forming a block. Rue de la Huchette still carries its 13th century name, and Rue du Chat-qui-Pêche is the narrowest street in Paris. This pedestrian quarter was the first to undergo renovation, and visitors should walk around looking upwards to admire the 17th century residences and narrow buildings with renovated façades that coexist harmoniously, giving the quarter a half-medieval, half-Bourbon feel. A charming church known as Saint-Julien-le-Pauvre, with a history similar to Saint-Séverin, stands on the other side of Rue Saint-Jacques. It, too, was built on a 6th century site, but its construction was prompted by its location at the intersection of the roads to Lyon and Orleans. Saint-Julien evokes a number of religious figures by that name, including Saint-Julien l'Hospitalier.

Indeed, the site once held a hostel for pilgrims. The Normans destroyed the first building, and the Benedictine monks rebuilt the church and added a priory in the 12th century. Saint-Julien soon attracted a considerable audience, university lecturers moved there and used the building for general assemblies. Albertus Magnus, Dante, Villon and Rabelais were frequent visitors. Unfortunately, in 1524, when students did not agree with the rector appointed by the university, they ransacked the church. It was closed during the Revolution, then opened again in 1826 when it was restored. At the end of the 19th century, it became an Eastern Orthodox church.

To the east of Saint-Julien-le-Pauvre, there is a homogeneous quarter with narrow streets at right angles to the quays, full of large mansions and apartment buildings. The most famous street is Rue de Bièvre, which was once used to divert water from a branch of the river by the same name to the gardens of the Abbey Saint-Victor. Here strollers will not find any flashy window displays.

University lectures were held outdoors at Place Maubert on Boulevard Saint-Germain, the stronghold of the famous Dominican monk, Master Albertus, a champion of Aristotle. When the "escholiers" or Schoolmen moved to Sainte-Geneviève hill, the square lost its lustre and was used as a place to torture heretics such as humanist Etienne Dolet. For a long time thereafter, "La Maube", as it came to be known, had a bad reputation.

Near the Sorbonne

Three buildings, located between Sainte-Geneviève hill and the Seine, stand out for historical reasons. The oldest is the Hôtel de Cluny, where two major periods in the history of Paris are represented by Gallo-Roman and medieval constructions which exist side by side in what was once the residence of the abbots of Cluny.

The Sorbonne is more famous. It is named after Robert de Sorbon, a monk from the Ardennes, who had once wished to study but had no money to do so. He bought a modest house with stables on this site and began teaching with only fifteen students. Soon, he was able to expand both his lands and his audience.

The Pantheon

Its history has much in common with the Madeleine church. Both buildings were commissioned by Louis XV and had an eventful history, but they ended up serving different opposite purposes: the Madeleine, a church without a cross, was finally used as a house of worship, whereas the Pantheon, with its Greek-cross plan surmounted by a very Christian-looking dome, is a "secular temple" (even though the Madeleine would have been better suited, given its exterior appearance). In 1885, after Victor Hugo's death, the etymology of the Pantheon (pan means everything, and theos means God) was rerouted when the monument was dedicated to "the great men", as inscribed on the pediment.

His college was reknowned for its moral rigor. Sorbon's successors kept this spirit, increasing the student body and even attracting foreigners.

The Collège de France was founded during the Renaissance by Guillame Budé, a humanist, in opposition to the "Sorbonnards" and their theology. Budé defended a return to regligious origins, rejecting the Church's use of Latin and scholasticism.

In 1530, Francis I inaugurated the "Collège des Trois Langues", where students learned Latin, Greek and Hebrew, and then Louis XIII added the "Collège Royal de France", which offered instruction in a wide variety of disciplines including medicine, mathematics, surgery, Arabic and astronomy.

Louis XVI put Chalgrin in charge of renovating the buildings and the name was changed to "Collège de France" during the Revolution. It has continued to offer lectures by renowned teachers such as Cuvier, Ampère, Renan, Valéry, Lacan and Braudel ever since.

The Latin Quarter presents a different face higher up on Sainte-Geneviève hill. It all started with the opposition of students and professors to the rigid authority of the Cité. They took refuge on the heights of the Left Bank, under the protection of the Abbey of Sainte-Geneviève, where the body of Clovis is buried.

The University was founded in the 12th century, with the support of Pope Innocent III, and it operated autonomously, with its own standards and rules. The church of Saint-Etienne-du-Mont, located next to the abbey church, drew its parishioners from all over the quarter. It was soon too small and had to be enlarged, but the work took more than a century.

Today visitors can admire the splendid interior with its flamboyant Gothic-style decorations, a rood screen (the last one built in Paris) and a Renaissance façade. Marguerite de Valois laid the cornerstone in 1610. Pascal and Racine are buried here.

Going down the hill, behind Saint-Etienne-du-Mont, the 5th arrondissement takes on the appearance of a market town. At the foot of the hill lies the former town of Saint-Médard, a very old quarter that was attached to the Abbey of Sainte-Geneviève early on. At the Place de la Contrescarpe, Rue Descartes turns into the picturesque Rue Mouffetard, once the road on which Romans set out to return home and which is now one of the most famous markets in Paris.

The church is somewhat overwhelmed by the immensity of the Pantheon, which dominates the square. It was erected in fulfilment of a vow made by Louis XV who promised to build it if he was cured. It was designed

by Soufflot who opened the wide street that bears his name to enhance the setting of the building and give it a beautiful view descending to the Luxembourg Gardens. He embellished the square with a law school. Across from it, Hittorff built a twin construction, the town hall of the 5th arrondissement.

The square also houses a building testifying to the iron architectural style of the 1850s. The Sainte-Geneviève library, designed by Labrouste, contains the precious manuscripts from the ancient Génovéfains Abbey, among others. The College de Montaigu, founded in the early 14th century, was once located on this site. Erasmus and Ignatius de Loyola often visited the establishment, which was famous for its austerity and mocked by Rabelais for its filth.

The Arena of Lutetia, located farther below, was discovered by chance during construction work that took place at the end of the 19th century.

The large amphitheatre, measuring 184 feet by 158 feet, was the setting for combat between gladiators and the martyrdom of Christians in fights with lions. During the 3rd century, it was destroyed by the Barbarians, and later on, Philippe Auguste used the stones to build his famous wall.

The quarter has been completely renovated in the direction of Val-de-Grace, but it has preserved the provincial atmosphere of the many convents found on its streets. Victor Hugo immortalized the convent that bears the name of the street where he lived during his childhood: Les Feuillantines.

The scenery changes abruptly after crossing the Rue Mouffetard, on the way to the Jardin des Plantes. The Mosque, built in the 1920s, appears with its shining white walls, evoking North Africa. It has its own *hammam* or steambath and a tearoom which are open to the public.

Going downhill, one comes to the Jardin des Plantes, which adds a bit of chlorophyll to a quarter that is singularly lacking in greenery.

The "Jardin des plantes medicinales" was created in 1626 by the doctors of Louis XIII. The area later became very fashionable during the reign of Louis XV. Buffon lived close by, and gave the garden a certain prestige by writing his *Histoire Naturelle*. The menagerie opened in 1793. Since then, it has continued its career as a Museum of Natural History.

The Institute of the Arab World is offers an elegant tribute to late 20th century architecture.

The Institute of the Arab World

The stunning architecture of this ultra-modern monument evokes recent university constructions in the emirates, and is a wonderful example of the symbiosis between traditional Arab art and avant-garde materials. The building, an extremely elegant and homogenous construction, presents exhibitions featuring varied aspects of Islamic culture and history.

Saint-Germain-des-Prés

Saint-Germain-des-Prés

The bell-tower is the only true vestige of Romanesque art in Paris, although the site had been chosen long before the development of this style. Childebert, the son of Clovis, agreed to lift the siege of the city of Saragossa in exchange for relics of the local patron saint, Saint Vincent. They finally came into his possession after many negotiations, and when he returned to France, he offered them to an abbey that had been created for the occasion in the countryside, to redeem himself for the assassination of his nephews. After Childebert's death, Bishop Germain dedicated the area to Saint Vincent, and it became the burial ground for the Merovingians and for Germain himself. The basilica was embellished sumptuously, with mosaics rivaling those of Ravenna, which were lost when the Normans laid waste to Paris without sparing the sanctuaries. When they were driven out, Paris was rebuilt and the abbey came to be known as Saint-Germain-des-Prés (Saint-Germain of the Meadows). Nine centuries later, the building still has one of its original bell-towers. The church was part of a Benedictine abbey, and the Romanesque builders rebuilt it according to the original plan, except for the nave. In 1950, Saint-Germain-des-Prés became famous worldwide when the existentialists moved into the cafés in the shadow of the bell-tower.

The fair and the market

Few of the covered markets that once gave Paris a wonderfully human warmth have been preserved. Multicoloured stalls full of fruit, vegetables and poultry, and the fragrance of spices and flowers attracted many enthusiasts.

Renovating this area at the heart of Saint-Germain-des-Prés caused a number of problems, but it was not the first time that the introducing changes here proved to be a thorny issue.

In 1813, Jean-Baptiste Blondel's decision to built the market of Saint-Germain provoked a stormy debate. Seven years earlier, Napoleon decreed the end of the Saint-Germain fair (already banned by the Revolution), which had existed since the Middle Ages. A charter dating from the late 12th century mentions the fair as a privilege granted to the Abbey of Saint-Germain-des-Prés. It spread out along the nearby streets, and was finally moved to Les Halles at the foot of the church of Saint-Eustache.

However, in 1482, the abbot of Saint-Germain-des-Prés wanted to improve his financial situation, and Louis IX allowed him the set up a a "free" market in the quarter.

The fair was an annual event that lasted about three weeks. It was so successful that it attracted all the commercial activity on the Left Bank. The Revolution, opposed to any sort of privilege, no longer allowed the clergy to hold the fair.

Nearly four hundred merchants took part in the fair. In addition to the stalls, there were as many different types of amusement available as there were people to enjoy them. Henri III is said to have strolled around the area with his mignons. Bear trainers, plays and puppets provided entertainment and animation, but the Royal Academy of Music and the Comédie-Française did not appreciate unfair competition, and a royal decree finally prohibited street actors from engaging in dialogue. The ingenious itinerant players wrote their texts in huge letters on rolls of paper and finally took to singing them. Comic opera was born.

The square

Paris takes pride in the number of "villages" that remained indifferent to rational Haussmannian street planning, and the contrasts on this square are among the most flagrant in the city.

On one side stands the sober Romanesque church (it was merely an abbey-church, whereas Saint-Sulpice was the parish church), and on the other side, a renowned café, Les Deux Magots, and next to it, another equally famous café, Le Flore.

The Brasserie Lipp is located on the opposite side of the Boulevard, untouched by time, where for years politicians trembled if the maître d'hotel failed to recognize or approve of them.

Saint-Germain-des-Prés church was built before Notre-Dame, but it has been altered and enhanced many times, and was damaged during the Revolution (in 1793, it served as a saltpeter factory). Seen from the outside, the building appears to be Romanesque, but inside there are many examples of Gothic art, especially the choirs.

The abbey palace of Charles de Bourbon is located near the church on Rue de l'Abbaye. It was built of brick and stone at the time of Henri III, and was virtually independent of the abbey.

The famous cafés, renowned since the 17th century, are located opposite the edifice.

The abbots of Saint-Germain-des-Prés encouraged artists to exhibit their works during the Saint-Germain fair. Coffee came into fashion during one of these events. An impoverished Sicilian aristocrat moved to Paris to make his fortune and entered a partnership with two Armenians who wished to introduce a new beverage at the fair. It proved so popular that he opened a first a small café and then a larger one at its current location: no. 13, Rue de l'Ancienne-Comédie.

The first Parisian café, the Procope, was born. It opened in 1684, opposite a hall where the Comédie-Française performed starting in 1689. Actors, encyclopaedists, writers and artists made it famous all over the world.

In the 1950s, disciples of existentialism gathered around Jean-Paul Sartre at the Saint-Germain cafés, where many writers spent their days composing novels.

On a street nearby, Rue Mazarine, a young actor named Molière set up his troupe in a royal tennis hall in 1643. Although he attracted huge crowds in the beginning, he lasted only a few months before his debts caught up with him.

After a second try, which was equally disastrous in financial terms, he decided to leave the city and spent a dozen years performing in villages in the provinces. When he returned to the capital, he met with success at last.

Two centuries later, Rue Visconti (now known as Rue du Marais Saint-Germain) was the site of another fiasco, when Balzac opened a printing press there. The business turned out to be a bottomless pit from a financial point of view, but at least it allowed him to describe the printing trade in meticulous detail in his novel *Lost Illusions*. Rue de Buci has been inhabited since the 14th century, and has always been a lively area.

In later years, it was the site of fashionable cafés, before becoming a busy commercial area.

Saint-Sulpice

Located a few yards away from a quarter that is lively by day as well as by night, the immediate neighborhood of the church of Saint-Sulpice is a timeless enclave, not unlike the area around the Vatican, where thousands of visitors dressed in full tourist regalia walk along, side by side with cassocked seminarians and nuns in cornets.

The current square used to be the site of the Grand Séminaire; the Petit Séminaire, located on Rue Férou, was reserved for students from modest families.

The establishments were closed at the time of the Revolution and torn down in 1802, only to be reconstructed during the Restoration. The seminarians were driven out again by a bill passed in 1906, and the

The square

At the foot of the famous bell-tower, this square is one of the most emblematic areas of Paris. Since the 19th century, Les Deux Magots, on the corner, and Le Flore, on Boulevard Saint-Germain, have been a magnet for writers and artists, and for a long time were considered literary sanctuaries. Maurras, Apollinaire, Prévert and Sartre and Simone de Beauvoir were all habitués of Le Flore.

state decided to set up offices of the Ministry of Finance in the building.

Today, the church dominates the large square. In the early 13th century, a small church stood on the site, which was used by the Parisians living in the Saint-Germain quarter. As the population increased, the church became too small. Anne of Austria laid the cornerstone for a new church. First Gamard, then Le Vau and, after his death, Gittard, were placed in charge of the works, which came to a halt in 1678 when the builders ran out of credit.

Oppenord continued the works thanks to winnings from the lottery, a frequent occurrence under the Old Regime. In 1733, Servandoni proposed a classical-style façade, which did not go very well with the Jesuit-style church.

The church towers were built in the middle of the 18th century by Maclaurin. They were given a rather unfavorable reception and were remodelled by Chalgrin, who only succeeded in reconstructing the tower on the left; the one on the right is Maclaurin's original construction.

Saint-Sulpice is one of the largest churches in Paris (360 feet long, 183 feet wide, 198 feet high). There are many secondhand bookshops and clothes shops in the vicinity, among them religious goods stores with windows displaying various models of chasables, ciboria, and religious images. Though some of the shops still smell of wax polish, they now have computerised cash registers. The quarter has retained the strong aura of a Catholic "bastion", which is confirmed by the large number of customers at "La Procure" bookshop.

Leaving Saint-Sulpice behind, we move on uphill towards the Odéon Theater, which turns its back to the Luxembourg Gardens. The names of the streets: de Condé, Monsieur-le-Prince (de Condé), Racine, Corneille, Crébillon, Médicis, Tournon and so on, all testify to the intellectual and historical aura of the quarter. Many writers chose to live in this area: Pascal wrote his *Les Provinciales* at 54 Rue Monsieur-le-Prince, George Sand lived on Rue Racine and Flaubert in Rue de l'Odéon. This last street, with all its secondhand bookshops, has no doubt preserved the most traditional atmosphere in the quarter.

When the Odéon Theater was built, it brought new liveliness to the quarter. The *Encylopédists* were particularly fond of this area.

Rue de Buci

This street joins Rue Dauphine and Rue de Seine. Though it has not yet been declared a pedestrian street, most passers-by, who are generally not very well disciplined, treat it as if it were one. The many shops at the foot of large 18th century buildings make the Rue de Buci a lively area for visitors and residents alike.

The quays

The 6th arrondissement gives onto the Seine by means of three prestigious quays, each one famous for a different reason.

Quai Malaquais. Some believe the etymology refers to the improper way in which Queen Margot acquired the land. The colourful Queen is responsible for the aristocratic air of the Left Bank. In 1605, when she already over fifty years old, the Queen granted her favors to a young squire who was killed by a rival. She had the rival beheaded but then began to loathe the Hôtel de Sens where she lived, and ordered the construction of a splendid palace opposite the Louvre, on Rue de Seine. To have her debts forgiven, she bequeathed her sumptuous palace with its enormous garden to Louis XIII. After his death, the palace was sold by plots, which started to bloom into private residences. The aristocrats loved the area, and stayed on, spreading out westward. Queen Margot's dissolute life did not stop her from being a generous queen (hence her debts) who always kept her promises. In 1608, she separated a piece of land from her large garden, and built a temple where young people continuously sang praises to the glory of Jacob; after a falling out, she replaced them with the Petits-Augustins. The convent was closed by the Revolution, and Alexandre Lenoir turned it into the Museum of French Monuments, which allowed him to save many works of art. Under the reign of Louis XVIII, it became the École des Beaux-Arts. The convent cloister was preserved, along with various architectural testimonies to other hôtels and the façacde of the Chateau d'Anet in the main courtyard on Rue Bonaparte.

Quai de Conti. Created long before its neighbor, this quay was reconstructed when the area behind Quai Malaquais was being built up. It used to house the Hôtel de Nesle, associated in local lore with the amorous affairs of the daughters-in-law of Philip the Fair. Two buildings stand out in the area: the French Institute and the Mint. The French Institute was built on the original site of the Porte de Nesle and the Mazarine Library where the Nesle tower once stood. Philippe Auguste's wall was torn down to make way for the construction. Since its creation, the Institute has maintained its prestige, and even today, being admitted under the Cupola of the Académie Française in the green uniform

Place Fürstenberg

This is one of the most charming squares in Paris, yet no single architect designed a masterpiece here, and the pink and white façade of the Abbey Palace standing at one end of the square contributes little or nothing to its atmosphere. The small square is full of trees and old-fashioned streetlamps and surrounded by white buildings. Delacroix lived and worked in his studio at no. 6. He loved "the joyful sunlight on the houses opposite my window" and "the view overlooking my small garden and the cheerful look of my studio." However, this did not stop him from speaking to the owner about the problems resulting from banning carriages in the square. He claimed this caused him great inconvenience when he went out at night or to the nearby Académie Française "in uniform", "when it was raining or the snow was melting". The square used to be the main courtyard of the Abbey Palace which was extended in the 18th century by Cardinal Egon de Fürstenberg.

In Rue de l'Ancienne-Comédie, all the shops and cafés have modern windows, except the Procope, which was recently remodelled in an old-fashioned style. Odéon Theater stands at the end of the street bearing the same name, in the center of a square that has not changed since 1799. The theater was built on land purchased by the king, who granted it to the City for a venue worthy of the Comédie-Française. The theater opened in 1782, closed during the Reign of Terror, and opened again in 1797 under the name the Odéon.

In 1915, Adrienne Monnier, a young woman from the provinces and a lover of old books, bought a bookshop on the Rue de l'Odéon with the compensation paid to her father for a work accident.

Thanks to its location in the book publishing quarter and the young owner's selfless devotion, the bookshop soon developed an extraordinary literary aura. When it opened in 1915, Paul Fort offered the owner a stock of unsold copies of his books, and Adrienne Monnier discovered she was in possession of a "treasure". The following year, Léon-Paul Fargue became a regular customer. Later on, numerous authors, including André Breton, Apollinaire and James Joyce, made "Shakespeare and Company", the bookshop owned by Adrienne Monnier and Sylvia Beach, an equally rare center of intellectual excitement.

reserved for members only constitutes the most prestigious of rewards. By accepting Marguerite Yourcenar, the institution proved it was eager to stay in touch with the times, unlike Richelieu who hoped, when it was created, that the French language would succeed "Latin, as Latin had succeeded Greek."

The other monument is the Hôtel des Monnaies or the Mint, built in 1768 by Louis XV to replace an old, dilapidated building. It was designed by an architect named Antoine who wished to distance himself from the trends of his time and used a sober, vaguely classical style. He created an innovative construction with a façade looking out over the Seine rather than perpendicular to it, as was the custom. The neighboring building, the Hôtel de Guénégaud, was a centre of wit and brilliance for Parisian aristocrats in the 17th century, typical of the constructions along the still untamed Seine. Mansart designed the splendid residence for Colbert's predecessor, where Racine and Boileau used to preview their writings.

The Quai des Grands-Augustins is on the other side of Rue Dauphine, once the most beautiful street in the capital. The quay was built on land belonging to monks, despite their vigorous protests.

The convent of the Grands-Augustins enjoyed considerable importance. It controlled all the Augustinian monks in France and its buildings sometimes housed secular meetings, such as Parliament, and the large hall was used to proclaim the regency of Marie de Medecis.

In the streets behind it, which in some cases date back to the 12th century, there still reigns an atmosphere of discreet charm. The *hôtels particuliers*, some of which were built in the 15th century, still have their splendid wrought-iron decorations.

The vast mansion belonging to the Duchesse d'Etampes, built for her by her royal lover François I, used to stand on Rue Gît-le-Coeur. The quarter grows lively again as soon as one reaches Rue Saint-André-des-Arts.

The French Institute cupola

The cupola is used for official meetings of the Académie Française, the oldest of the five French academies. In March 1634, Richelieu agreed to sponsor a small group of men of letters who used to meet at the Conrart bookshop. After his death, Mazarin bequeathed two million books for the instruction of some sixty promising students from the recently conquered provinces of France (Piedmont, Alsace, Artois and Roussillon). In 1684, Le Vau drew up plans for the Collège des Quatre-Nations, on the site of the Hôtel de Nesle, and in 1805, Napoleon moved the five academies that made up the Institute from the Louvre to this site.

Luxembourg and the Senate

The Luxembourg Palace is currently the seat of the Senate, whose members are chosen by a college composed of members of parliament, regional councillors and municipal representatives. The Senate is the guardian of the Constitution, shares legislative power with the French National Assembly, and its president acts as president of the Republic in an emergeny situation. The "Petit Luxembourg", which used to be the Hôtel du Luxembourg, is the residence of the Senate president.

The large park is officially owned by the senators, who are appointed for nine-year terms, but it is open to the public. Here one can stroll among a wide variety of visitors, from children playing or guiding their toy sailboats to students reading.

The park is laid out as a French-style garden, except for a series of narrow English-style paths. It was planned in the 17th century on land that once belonged to an old monastery. It was redesigned in accordance with English-style architecture in the 19th century, and decorated with a number of statues and monuments, some of which are more interesting than others. The most attractive is the Medicis Fountain built by Salomon de Brosse in 1624, with sculptures recalling mythological episodes. This is the largest and most famous garden on the Left Bank. It was created by Marie

de Medicis when she built her palace. It became very fashionable during the 18th century, and Watteau and Diderot loved strolling along its paths.

In Gallo-Roman times, the Luxembourg area was occupied by villas and a camp that were destroyed by invasions of Barbarians and Huns. King Robert the Pious, who ruled from 970 and 1035, ordered the construction of the "Chateau Vauvert". Legend has it that the castle was abandoned and later haunted. In 1257, the Carthusian monks of Chantilly had to exorcise the spot and then built a convent famed for its flower nursery and kitchen garden.

After Henri IV's death, Marie de Medicis no longer wanted to stay at the Louvre and called upon the architect Salomon de Brosse to design a palace inspired by the Pitti Palace in Florence, where she was born. She bought the Duke de Luxembourg's residence in 1612, and the construction works began in 1615. Rubens decorated the sumptuous mansion with a series of twenty-four large allegorical paintings recounting the life of Marie de Medicis. (They are currently on display at the Louvre).

The plan of the palace was French, but its décor was Italian, with rustication, fluted columns and Tuscan capitals. Marie did not enjoy her palace for long, as she had to flee to Cologne after the Day of the Dupes

Luxembourg Palace

This splendid 17th century construction was commissioned by Marie de Medicis, and it gives us a good idea of the architectural style at the time of Louis XIII. Marie, the widow of Henri IV, put the architect Salomon de Brosse in charge of building a residence reminiscent of the Pitti Palace in Florence. The mansion was to remind her of her birthplace, but the architect complied only partially with her wishes and Italy was somewhat forgotten in the plans. Marie de Medecis is said to have been an enthusiast of esotericism and the precise geometry of the plans of the Luxembourg Place may have an occult meaning. An analysis of the plan indded reveals that the axis is oddly perpendicular to the Louvre.

(November 10, 1630). After the death of her son, Louis XIII, in 1643, the Luxembourg Palace went to Louis' brother, Gaston d'Orléans and then to his daughter "La Grande Mademoiselle".

It was inherited by Louis XIV who used it to accommodate distinguished guests, and in the 18th century the Duchess de Berry received the palace from her father, the Regent, though she was not wealthy enough to maintain it. The authorities took it over and set up France's first art museum within its walls. The King himself lent some of his paintings from the Palace of Versailles to be displayed there.

When the Carthusian convent was closed in 1790, the park was extended and the Avenue de l'Observatoire (leading to the Observatory) was created. The palace was renamed the House of National Security during the Reign of Terror (1793), and received Danton, Camille Desmoulins, Fabre d'Eglantine and Hébert.

Assemblies were held here under the Directoire and the Consulate. Chalgrin (1739-1811) remodeled the interior to suit its new purpose. He also designed the Observatory Gardens that extend from the Luxembourg gardens. Colbert was put in charge of building the Observatory according to plans by Charles Perrault.

The Medicis Fountain

This fountain is undoubtedly one of the dearest to the hearts of Parisians. Joseph Kessel named the first volume of Le tour du malheur, *in which he recounts his troubled youth, after the fountain. The Medici Fountain is a haven of cool and quiet for students lucky enough to be able to come here and read in fine weather.*

A Kiosk

This charming little kiosk reminds visitors that some places in Paris are oblivious to the passage of time. More than one hundred and twenty years ago, André Gide used to play with his hoop along the garden's paths.

Montparnasse

Towards the Observatory

Walking along Rue Auguste-Comte, away from the Luxembourg area, one comes upon the Rue d'Assas and the Notre-Dame quarter, which joins Montparnasse on the charming triangle formed by Rue Bréa and Rue Vavin. Towards the left, the long Rue Saint-Jacques climbs up, parallel to Boulevard Saint-Michel. Here, a military hospital and a museum now occupy the buildings that were once the Benedictine abbey of Val-de-Grace. The church was built to fulfil a vow made by Anne of Austria, who promised to build a church if she bore Louis XIII an heir. Young Louis XIV laid the cornerstone in 1645. This is the only Parisian abbey that has preserved all of its 17th century buildings.

The ancient Jansenist abbey of Mother Angélique Arnault and Jacqueline, Pascal's sister, was located at 121 Boulevard Port-Royal. The church and the main building are still intact. The next building is the Observatory. Louis XIV asked Perrault to design it and

placed Colbert in charge of its construction, with a view to encouraging astronomy. Its four sides correspond to the four cardinal points. No iron was used in the construction of the building to avoid interference. The south side became the latitude of Paris, and the meridian passes through the middle of the building.

Montparnasse

This quarter is named for Parnassus, the mountain of the Muses, which the Ancient Greeks once dedicated to Apollo. It was the sacred place of the poets.

Stone quarries were mined on this site in Roman times and windmills operated here during the Middle Ages. The quarter came to life with the arrival of the railway, which brought the Bretons to Paris. Craftsmen and industries such as the Bréguet factory blossomed in the area.

However, it was the artists who made the area famous, creating a real boom around 1910 when they left Montmartre and moved to Montparnasse. A complex of artists' studios called *La Ruche* (The Hive), located on the Passage de Danzig, opened in the early 20th century, and many of the artists that made the Bateau-Lavoir famous came down from the hill to this new area. Soon, there were studios all over the quarter inhabited by artists, sculptors and models who filled the cafés in the neighborhood.

As in Montmartre, artists came from all over the world and worked in every discipline: writers and musicians joined the recently arrived painters. Paul Fort and Francis Carco made the café La Closerie des Lilas fashionable, and Apollinaire, Modigliani, Zadkine and Foujita frequented La Rotonde. Picasso played an important role in the choice of the new artistic center, along with Jarry, Derain, Salmon and Max Jacob. A new generation appeared from 1918 to the 1930s: Cocteau, Cendrars, Breton, Miró, Max Ernst, Matisse, and Giacometti. Among the musicians were Erik Satie, Stravinsky, and the Paris Six (Honegger, Auric, Milhaud, Poulenc, Durey and Taillefer).

The Institute of Art and Archaeology

The architectural style of this building does not please everyone. It is not really located in the Montparnasse quarter, although it is typical of 1930s, when Montparnasse was in full bloom. To the left and right of the Boulevard Montparnasse, there were many streets filled with artists' studios including Rue de la Grand-Chaumière, Rue Campagne-Première, Rue Bréa, etc. This building currently houses the Jacques-Doucet Library.

Hemingway and Henry Miller joined in on the fun. Meanwhile, other more discreet foreigners, such as Russian refugees who had just led a revolution (Lenin and Trotsky among them), moved from the cafés of Paris, such as the Dôme, to the halls of the Kremlin.

Montparnasse is still a lively quarter in the shadow of a 656-foot tower.

In 1974, the now famous tower replaced the old Montparnasse railway station, which moved a few yards uphill and now accomodates high-speed train traffic to the Atlantic coast. The building of the new station led to created profound and often harshly criticized architectural upheaval in the quarter.

Ricardo Bofill, which offer an interesting example of avant-garde architecture. This new Paris is cold and abstract, despite the fact that the old streets, packed tightly together along the city's western cemetery, were often often insalubrious.

The Boulevard Raspail was finally finished and inaugurated by President Poincaré in 1913. The Cité Nicolas-Poussin, located between numbers 240-242, grouped together the houses of artists and their half-timbered studios. In 1865 Emile Trélat founded the Special School of Architecture; the school's garden contains columns from the Tuileries castle that was burned down in 1871.

Moving on from Boulevard Edgar-Quinet, which balances its busy daytime market with popular theatres at night, one comes upon what was once a lively, working-class quarter extending to Place Denfert-Rochereau and the Porte d'Orléans. This was the Paris of small shop-keepers (the Rue Daguerre has preserved this atmosphere), an animated, friendly area with modest houses that were still affordable in a calm, traditional neighborhood. Most of it was demolished during the renovation process initiated twenty years ago, and many residents had to leave. Today, the newly rehabilitated section covers a wide area, including the Place de Catalogne, lined with elegant buildings designed by

For a long time, the American Center for Students and Artists was located at number 261, in a building where Chateaubriand lived from 1826 to 1838. Artists' studios were found on Rue Campagne-Première: Picasso and Miró lived at no. 3, Kandinsky at no. 9 and the photographer Atget at no. 17.

At the far end of the 14th arrondissement, the students living in dormitories at the Cité Universitaire can take advantage of the greenery at Montsouris Park, with its sloping hill, adorned with waterfalls and a lake. The Bardo, a replica of the palace of the beys in Tunisia, had embellished the park since the 1867 World Fair but burned down in 1991.

An artist's studio in Montparnasse

This photograph was published in the New York Herald in 1934, and is quite representative of the mood in Montparnasse at the time. This is the Institute of Contemporary Aesthetics, located at no. 86, Rue Notre-Dame-des-Champs, and run by Paul Bornet. Here, wealthy Americans worked side by side with socialites and young art students such as Foujita. It is interesting to note that the men surrounding the nude model are all wearing suits and ties.

The Saint-Germain quarter

"What is known in France as the Faubourg Saint-Germain quarter is neither a district nor a sect nor an institution, nor something that can be clearly explained. In relation to Paris, its customs and manner of speaking, in short, the Faubourg Saint-Germain tradition, is today what the Court used to be." The preceding description, from *La Duchesse de Langeais*, published in the early 19th century, was Balzac's definition of a district that has been considerably diminished over the years. The number of *hôtels particuliers* has dropped from two hundred to fifty, and the remaining ones house ministries and embassies rather than aristocratic families. However, even a hundred and fifty years after their were built, they still retain an almost mythical prestige.

All the same, the fact that ministers live and work in these old mansions may account for their continuing prestige. Senior officials with degrees from the School of Political Science and the School of Public Administration, located on Rue Saint-Guillame, Rue des Saints-Pères and Rue de Lille, now perform their functions a few yards away in identical private mansions on Rue de Grenelle, Rue Saint-Dominque, Rue Las Cases, Rue Barbet-de-Jouy, Rue de Varenne, etc. Political mutations have left the quarter unchanged. The heavy doors of the *hôtels particuliers* have kept their aura, and even the Russian Embassy on the Rue de Grenelle never lost its the aristocratic atmosphere during the Soviet era.

In the earlier, pleasure-loving era of the Czars, that same residence was guarded by two Cossacks in costume, who looked on as guests entered a sort of Ali Baba's cave or rather, what the French imagined a Russian party must be like, with gypsies singing, Cossacks dancing and vodka flowing to wash down the caviar. A hundred and fifty years later, the atmosphere was essentially the same.

In this quarter, between Boulevard Saint-Germain and Les Invalides, everything is elegant, sober, discreet and perhaps even a bit cold. The area is relatively new, although today it is often assumed to be part of an older one, with *hotels particuliers* dating from the 17th century, in the vicinity of the ancient Abbey of Saint-Germain-des-Prés.

The first person to make this part of the Left Bank famous was the legendary Queen Margot. Some say she acquired the marshland that became Quai Malaquais illegally, hence the name *mal acquis* (wrongly acquired). Others say the name refers to the marsh that made it difficult for boats to dock (*mal à quai*). In the 18th century, aristocrats chose the area to build their large mansions, and financiers and ambassadors joined in the round of receptions and literary salons. This society life was interrupted by the Revolution, but it started up again during the Restoration and came back into fashion in the 1880s.

Palais-Bourbon

Today, the Palais-Bourbon is a symbol of democracy. The deputies who meet in Parliament represent the people of France; each one is elected directly by voters from a district. The palace takes its name from the Duchesse de Bourbon, a woman who evokes a far less democratic tradition, which allowed French kings to legitimize some of their bastard offspring. The Duchesse de Bourbon was the daughter of Louis XIV and Madame de Montespan.

Giardini and Lassurance began the construction works, which were finished by Aubert and Gabriel years later. In 1756, Louis XV bought the palace, with a view to developing the square that bore his name (now known as Place de la Concorde), located across the river. The Prince de Condé bought back the building in 1764 and had it transformed, extended and luxuriously decorated. He even ordered the construction of the Place du Palais-Bourbon, which was to be surrounded by identical houses that would make the entrance to his mansion on Rue de l'Université, even more majestic. The square has remained unchanged.

The Revolutionaries took over this rather ostentatious royal symbol. In 1795, it was donated to the French Council of Five-Hundred and the architects Gisors and Lecomte transformed its splendid salons into assembly rooms.

The Rodin Museum

Rodin lived in this 18th century mansion for about twenty years. He negotiated with the state (which owned the building) and declared that he would leave all of his works to the city if he was allowed to live on the property. Thus, it became a museum, inaugurated in 1919, two years after his death. The Biron mansion displays a vast collection of paintings, sketches and sculptures. Some of Rodin's most famous works, such as the statue of Balzac and the bronze version of The Thinker, *shown on the opposite page, are exhibited in the gardens.*

Napoleon wanted one of the National Assembly façades to look out over the Place de la Concorde, so from 1804 to 1807, Poyet built a classical façade with twelve Corinthian columns surmounted by a pediment. At the same time, Napoleon ordered the construction work at the Madeleine on a temple dedicated to the France's Great Army to be continued. He wanted the two building façades to be symmetrical. The Prince de Condé decided to rent the Assembly building to the state and live in the adjoining mansion, the Hôtel de Lassay, which is now the residence of the president of the French National Assembly. The neoclassical building familiarly known as the "Quai d'Orsay", where the French Ministry of Foreign Affairs is housed, is a relatively recent construction: the Doric columns were built during the Second Empire. At night, when seen from the quays, the three succeeding buildings look particularly elegant.

Hôtel Matignon

This is the most beautiful mansion in the quarter. It has belonged to the Prime Minister since January 1959. While political fluctuations regularly lead to a change in the official occupant, the ins and outs of alliances and successions have have also influenced the list of former occupants. In that respect, the mansion stands out from others in this aristocratic area, where for a long time an aura of continuity reigned, with some families owning their mansions for over a century. The main entrance is located at 57 Rue de Varenne, but the superb gardens extend to the Rue de Babylone.

Originally, the hôtel of the Baron de Pouancé stood here. It was demolished by the son of the Maréchal de Luxembourg, an eccentric who lived off his wife's fortune (she was the daughter of Harlay, the Comte de Beaumont). Courtonne was put in charge of reconstructing the building. The unpredictable owner, a Maréchal de France, sold the unfinished building to Jacques de Matignon in 1723. The latter's son married the daughter of the Prince de Monaco, who left her his debts along with his title. The construction works started up again. In 1751, the Comte de Matignon's grandson inherited the mansion when he became the ruling Prince de Monaco after his mother's death. The mansion was confiscated during the Reign of Terror, but was later

returned to the family who then sold it. Talleyrand bought it in 1808. For three years, he lived a life of luxury here and his magnificent receptions were partly financed by the Emperor. In 1811, the state bought the mansion when he left and moved to Rue Saint-Florentin. Later, Louis XVIII exchanged it for the Elysée Palace, which then belonged to the Duchesse de Bourbon. It is interesting to note that today the French Republic uses the old Bourbon *hôtels particuliers* as residences for the country's president, prime minister and the National Assembly, and has admirably preserved the splendor of these buildings.

Saint-Thomas-d'Aquin

This small, discreet parish used to be the novitiate chapel of the Dominican monks. It was built by Pierre Bullet, a student of Blondel, who followed in his master's footsteps while producing more massive works. Oddly enough, the church that Bullet built for the Dominicans was insired by the church of Gesu, the architectural model of the Jesuits, who were the competitors of the Dominicans. The Revolution abolished the Dominican convent, and turned it into the parish of Saint-Thomas-d'Aquin in 1791. The buildings that once belonged to the convent were transferred to the Army.

Sainte-Clotilde

Cornered between Rue de Grenelle and Rue Saint-Dominique, this small basilica is located at the end of the beautiful Rue Las Cases, and stands in odd contrast to the mansions in the quarter. Its neo-Gothic architecture, which is especially visible behind Les Invalides, has generated considerably criticism. The building was planned during the Restoration, although the works did not begin until the end of the July Monarchy, with the support of Marie-Amélie. Until World War I, the parish registers recorded all the baptisms, marriages and burials in the the Faubourg, providing an account of the births, alliances and inheritance of its residents.

Hôtel de Seignelay

This mansion was built by Boffrand and was used by Colbert's son, the Marquis de Seignelay. It was later bought by the Duc de Charost, an eccentric character, who set up a philanthropic society in his luxurious home. The building was erected during the 18th century and still retains its noble atmosphere, which corresponds to the golden age of the quarter and the mentality of its residents. Like the Hôtel de Beauharnais, this mansion has an advantage over other buildings in the quarter: they both have sober entrances, but once the heavy doors are closed and one climbs the steps, the view overlooking the Seine is magnificent.

The Palace
of the Legion of Honor

The Hôtel de Salm was built in 1782 by Pierre Rousseau, and is a rather late construction compared to other buildings in the quarter. The mansion has a curious history. It was built by the wealthy Prince de Salm, but he lived in the residence as his architect's tenant, since he could not pay his bill. The building was erected in a place known as "La Grenouillière", a large wasteland reaching to the river bank. Rousseau took advantage of the expanse of the land to design magnificent gardens. Despite his financial problems, the Prince de Salm led a sumptuous life in the mansion and his parties were a model of the 18th-century art of good living. When the Revolution took place, he was elected deputy of Lorraine in the Constituent Assembly, but his public image did not improve and he was unable to escape the guillotine. The mansion was then used for the constitutional club under Madame de Staël. In 1804, it became the property of the Great Chancellery of the Legion of Honor which now uses it as a museum. It was destroyed by a fire in 1871, and reconstructed in a widely criticized neoclassical style. The colonnade recalls the neighboring Palais-Bourbon, although this construction stands out from the sober colonnades of the mansions often hidden behind austere entrances.

Ecole Libre
des Sciences Politiques

The School of Political Science, known as "Sciences Po" represents the good and ill fortunes of the French political class, for all of the country's senior officials and almost all of its ministers, regardless of their political stripe, have attended this institution.

The peaceful gardens of the old Hôtel de Mortemart have witnessed generations of young people forge their minds under the tutelage of their teachers Emile Boutmy and André Siegfried. Many institutions have modelled themselves on the School of Political Science, not only in London and Harvard but also in Cairo and Athens.

Hôtel de Beauharnais

This beautiful mansion was the source of many family disputes. Napoleon was outraged by the expenses run up by Prince Eugene, Empress Josephine's son. In retrospect, one can only rejoice at the Prince's taste. Thanks to him, we have an prime example of Empire period splendor. Some rooms, such as a bathroom, exhibit the new trend at the time: a revival of the style of Ancient Egypt.

Orsay Museum

The Orsay palace was built during the July Monarchy, and was the seat of the Government Accounting Office and the Council of State. It was destroyed by fire during the fighting between the Versailles soldiers and the federated National Guard of the Commune in 1871, and remained in ruins until preparations began for the World Fair in 1900, when it was converted into a railway station.

The architect Victor Laloux studied the plans of the Paris-Orléans railway company engineers, and promptly began the works. Two years later, on July 14, 1900, the leading personalities of Paris attended the inauguration of the station and the luxurious adjoining mansion. A number of major events took place at Orsay. On May 19, 1958, General de Gaulle held a press conference to announce that he was about to take power. Orson Welles filmed various scenes of *The Trial* here. In 1973, the Orsay palace became the the Renaud-Barrault theater, where Madeleine Renaud gave a legendary performance in *Oh les beaux jours*. The Hôtel Drouot auction house also occupied the premises for a few years.

In 1973, a project was put forward to convert the railway station into a hotel complex. The management of the Museums of France proposed instead a museum that would display works created between 1848 and 1914, thus creating a link between the artwork displayed in the Louvre and the Georges-Pompidou Centre (Beaubourg). The project was finally approved by Valéry Giscard d'Estaing. The architectural studies were carried out by R.Bardon, P.Colboc and J.-P. Philippon. François Mitterand inaugurated the museum in 1986. The decision was made to preserve the iron structure typical of turn-of-the-century architecture, to avoid the protests generated by the destruction of the glass pavillions in Les Halles created by Baltard. It is not easy to transform a train station into a museum, and Gae Aulenti used stone to decorate the interior of the large "nave" and provide a setting for sculptures, marbles and bronzes. It was a huge success: by 1987, it had already received almost four million visitors. In 1988, the temporary exhibitions displaying Van Gogh's Parisian paintings and Cézanne's early works, attracted eight hundred thousand people.

Inside

To the right of the square, there are six statues representing the continents (South and North America each have a statue). The ground floor displays the works of artists from Rude to Carpeaux. On the right-hand side, Ingres (The Spring), Delacroix (The Lion Hunt), alongside academic painters (Gérôme, Chassériau, Winterhalter, Cabanel, Clésinger, Thomas Couture). Realism is featured on the left-hand side with Daumier (The Washerwoman), Millet (The Angelus, The Gleaners), Corot (The Dance of the Nymphs) and the Barbizon painters (Théodore Rousseau, Daubigny, Troyon), Courbert (A Burial at Ornans, The Studio). Then Puvis de Chavannes (The Poor Fisherman), the symbolist Gustave Moreau (Jason and Orpheus) and works created before 1870 by Degas (The Opera Orchestra), Manet (Olympia, Picnic on the Grass), Monet (Women in the Garden), Bazille (Family Reunion), and Renoir. Impressionist pioneers: Boudin and Jongkind and landscapes by Sisley and Pissarro. On the middle floor, there are sculptures by Rodin (The Age of Bronze, Balzac), Camille Claudel (The Age of Maturity) and Maillol (Desire). Decorative arts are also displayed, and there is a section for jewellery, furniture and pottery. Matisse (Luxury, calm and delight), Douanier Rousseau (The Snake Charmer), Klimt and Munch are grouped in a small room. The top floor is dedicated to the prestigious Impressionist collection of: Monet, Manet, Renoir, Pissarro, and Sisley. There are also paintings by Degas, Berthe Morisot and Caillebotte and the independent works of Van Gogh, Gaugin, Cézanne and Toulouse-Lautrec, pointillist paintings by Seurat and Signac, works by the Nabi painters (Maurice Denis, Pierre Bonnard, Vuillard) and Le Douanier Rousseau.

Les Invalides and the Champ-de-Mars

Les Invalides

Louis XIV was thirty-two years old when he ordered the construction of the Hôtel des Invalides. The King wanted to solve a problem that his predecessors, Henri IV and Louis XIII, had also confronted: what should be done with disabled veterans? The War of Devolution has just ended; he knew he would need his people to fight in other wars and decided it was essential to enhance the role of the soldier, as there was nothing more demoralizing and unjust in the eyes of the population than the sight of wounded and disabled soldiers abandoned to their fate.

He ordered this superb mansion to be built and named it after the unfortunate soldiers: Les Invalides. The building was a reflection of his kingdom: immense and superb. He laid the cornerstone on November 30, 1670, and put Libéral Bruant, who had built Salpétrière Hospital for the poor ten years earlier, in charge of construction. The architect took his inspiration from the Escurial palace built a century earlier. The construction was completed by Hardouin-Mansart.

The vast square of Les Invalides is more than 1,500 feet long and 800 feet wide, and houses six main courtyards. The façade is 688 feet long. Like the Escurial, the complex is as majestic as it is austere and geometrical. It would have been completely different if Hardouin-Mansart had been able to carry out his plan and create a colonnade around his superb dome.

The main entrance is not on the Esplanade but on the other side, on Place Vauban, in the centre of a round colonnade similar to the one Bernini created for Saint Peter's Square in Rome.

There are many reasons to visit Les Invalides. First there is the Esplanade itself, an extension of the Pont Alexandre III, offering a splendid view. It was created by Robert de Cotte who carried out the works during the beginning of the 18th century on land that belonged in part to the Pré-aux-Clercs.

There is a large garden in front of the mansion, which is closed in by a gate and ditches with cannons captured from enemies. The main courtyard is reached through an entrance in the centre of the long façade. The entrance is surmounted by a monumental triumphal arch which covers the four floors of the façade. An equestrian statue of Louis XIV as a Roman warrior by Guillaume Coustou decorates the frontispiece. The famous dome is perfectly aligned in the overall view.

The church known as Saint-Louis or the Soldier's Church, is located at the far end of the main courtyard. This long, narrow construction was created before the dome. The clergy did not allow arms inside their churches, but they were not opposed to using flags as decorations. The construction possesses two magnificent organs, and the Army set up a museum of military history within the walls.

Finally, there is the church of the Dôme, Hardouin-Mansart's masterpiece, which many people consider the most perfect example of French architecture. He embellished his uncle's plans by gracefully combining baroque and classical styles.

He created a church with a Greek cross plan and small proportions which he decorated with a combination of every style. On the outside, the chapels leading to the choir create four sections elevated to two floors. Hardouin-Mansart created a highly "personalized" main entrance: Corinthian columns surmounted by a triangular frontispiece. The dome rests on the main floor, and is lit by twelve windows and an attic. It is made of gilded lead, adorned with countless trophies.

Inside, Charles de Lafosse represented the four evangelists and, on the second cupola, he painted Saint Louis offering Christ a sword. Hardouin-Mansart, Robert de Cotte and Charles de Lafosse were artists from Versailles whom Louis XIV "lent" for the construction of this royal residence which he so much desired.

Only soldiers who had served for at least ten years were accommodated in the mansion. Following the revocation of the Edict of Nantes, Protestants had to renounce their faith in order to be admitted. The rules allowed pensioners to work. A century after it was created, the institution was the pride of the regime, and on July 14, 1789, the people entered the building in search of arms and came away with almost thirty thousand weapons.

The dome of Les Invalides

This magnificent dome was re-gilded during the festivities marking the Bicentenary of the French Revolution. The celebration offered an opportunity to refurbish some of the monuments in the capital. The dome on this church is one of Hardouin-Mansart's masterpieces. Soldiers say that a war breaks out every time the dome is re-gilded. Two years after the last restoration, the French army sent its troops to Kuwait.

Ecole Militaire

Les Invalides was built during the reign of Louis XIV, and his minister of war, Louvois, encouraged him greatly in this enterprise. Louis XV ordered the construction of the Ecole Militaire during his reign, and the project was backed by his mistress, Madame de Pompadour, and a financier friend, Pâris-Duverney. Like Louis XIV before him, he put his architects from Versailles in charge of the project; Gabriel succeeded Hardouin-Mansart and Libéral Bruant, although the latter never actually built anything at Versailles. Louis XIV provided housing for almost three thousand injured soldiers; Madame de Pompadour suggested that Louis XV train five hundred impecunious gentlemen for a period of three years, to turn them into perfect strategists. There were thus connections between the two military constructions located close to each other on what used to be the Plain of Grenelle, and one could draw up a long list of the similarities and differences between them, especially at a distance of two centuries.

The most obvious fact is that the 17th century bequeathed us Les Invalides, a sober yet magnificent classical monument, and the 18th did the same with a small, surprising luxurious building a mere army barracks. Gabriel had to be restrained from excessive spending, as he would willingly have added further embellishments to his construction.

Nowadays, the public is allowed to visit Les Invalides but not the Ecole Militaire, whose splendid chapel is only opened for special occasions. The School currently offers university-level military training for officers.

The Ecole Militaire is proud to have had a famous alumnus, Napoleon Bonaparte, even though his instructors failed to judge him correctly, for they predicted he would have a brilliant career in the Navy. He entered the military school when he left the College de Brienne, in 1784; the Ecole Militaire had become an Advanced School for Cadets in 1777, after having been disbanded in 1776.

The school was abolished in 1787, and the Revolutionaries ransacked the building. In the middle of the 19th century, it was turned into military barracks, and a series of imposing constructions were annexed along the façade giving onto the Champ-de-Mars. Gabriel's palace lost its elegance, although in 1878 it became the seat of the National School of War. In 1944, the tanks of Lerclerc's division drove the Germans from the premises. The Military School has recovered its educational role once again; it also houses the only military riding school in the centre of Paris.

Napoleon's tomb at Les Invalides

The church of the Dôme is currently dedicated to the memory of the Emperor. The transfer of his body from Saint Helena led to numerous transactions and was the occasion for a surprisingly fertile artistic boom. Many artists presented their projects, and Visconti's design was chosen. He created a large tomb made of red porphyry resting on a large base of green Vosges granite which would be displayed in the crypt in the church of the Dôme. The interior area of the building was thoroughly remodeled. A circular hole was cut in the floor so as to open up the space all the way to the dome, creating a stunning effect. Members of the imperial family are buried on the ground floor, and on December 15, 1940, Hitler sent the body of l'Aiglon (Napoleon's son, known as the "Eaglet"), who had been buried alongside the Hapsburgs.

Opposite page:
The old Flag Room

The Invalides mansion houses one of the most complete military museums in the world. In this room, a great number of flags, some French and some captured from enemy armies, evoke the military side of French history.

53

The Eiffel Tower and the Champ-de-Mars

The Champ-de-Mars was planned as grounds for military maneuvers. Until then, it was called the Plain of Grenelle and had been used for growning vegetables. As soon as the tracks were laid out, the first horse race was held. Peculiar ceremonies took place here during the Revolution. Talleyrand acted as an unexpected officiating priest and celebrated the Federation mass on July 14, 1790, as the last hope for reconciliation.

Four years later, Robespierre used the field to celebrate the Feast of the Supreme Being. The field was then used as the grounds for a series of World Fairs; five of them were held in little more than half a century. The 1878 fair, which was intended to prove that France was back on its feet economically after the debacle of 1870, was highly successful. A World Fair was organized to celebrate the first centenary of the French Revolution in 1889. It was a brilliant display that left behind a revolutionary construction: the Eiffel Tower.

Located in the area close to the Seine at the end of the Champ-de-Mars, the tower was designed by Gustave Eiffel and has become the symbol of Paris, replacing Notre-Dame in the iconography representing the capital.

The idea of building a tower had been in the air for a number of years. In 1833, an English engineer had studied the possibility of a 984-foot tower (as tall as the Eiffel Tower), but he died before he could build it. In 1884, engineers succeeded in erecting a 554-foot tower in Washington, and in 1885, the first skyscraper was built in Chicago.

The leaders of the Third Republic decided to provide the capital with an unrivaled construction that would demonstrate France's industrial power and impress the world. They were looking for a construction that would stand out for the originality of its design and appearance. Gustave Eiffel's project was chosen because it was the most feasible and the most carefully engineered out of approximately one hundred plans that were presented. Thus, an expert in iron constructions won the competition, and in two years (1887-1889), he built a masterpiece of technology which still stands a century later. Gustave Eiffel designed a 554 feet tower, and needed about 300 erectors (acrobats, one could say)

to raise this 7,000-ton construction, consisting of 15,000 iron pieces held together with 2,500,000 rivets. Inside, 1,652 steps lead up to the top of the tower.

The "Protest of the Three Hundred" composed by Maupassant, Garnier, Gounod, Leconte de Lisle, Dumas the younger, François Coppée, etc. opposed the construction, which they thought did not conform to the tasteful architectural buildings created in Paris after the Renaissance. Despite the opposition, the Eiffel Tower generated wild enthusiasm during the World Fair in 1889 and many artists have praised the tower, such as writers

The Eiffel Tower in springtime

Before the construction of the Ecole Militaire, the Champ-de-Mars was only used for growing vegetables. Gabriel designed a large plain for military maneuvers, and the area was opened to the public. In 1790, Talleyrand celebrated a strange mass during the Feast of the Federationin his capacity as a constitutional bishop. Three years later, Robespierre presided over the Feast of the Supreme Being. After the Directoire period, the land was used for World Fairs. Eiffel erected his tower in 1889, as the star of the fair that year. Architects built many elegant apartment buildings and private mansions with enclosed gardens all around the Champ-de-Mars. Despite early opposition to the Eiffel Tower, it is still standing today, and attracts millions of tourists every year. At the foot of the tower, near the Seine, the English-style gardens are refreshingly cool in the summer, whereas at the Ecole Militaire, the grass in the French-style gardens is often subjected to blazing sunlight.

like Apollinaire and Cocteau (*Les Mariés de la Tour Eiffel*) and painters such as Pissarro, Dufy, Utrillo and Delaunay.

The Eiffel Tower that has become the symbol of Paris was originally supposed to be torn down twenty years after the World Fair. However, in 1909 it proved to have a scientific use. It was used in various experiments related to communication and broadcasting, and in 1957, it was finally enshrined when a television antenna was placed on top of the tower, and meteorology and air navigation stations were created inside.

With the antenna, the Eiffel Tower now rises to 1,052 feet. The last World Fair was celebrated in 1937 on the grounds in front of Les Invalides and the Champ-de-Mars, but mostly on the Right Bank at Palais de Chaillot and the Palais de Tokyo.

Steel architecture was in fashion during the exhibition, and all the delegations prided themselves on having produced the most beautiful pavilion.

The Soviet delegation stood opposite the Nazi pavilion; neither one was particularly pleased, as they both claimed this honor.

THE RIGHT BANK

Place de la Bastille

It may seem odd to start our journey along the Right Bank at the Place de la Bastille, but since this is a geographical tour, the Bastille is the first complex of monuments that appears in the east of the capital.

The project and construction of a modern opera house in the Place de la Bastille gave rise to many questions then (and perhaps still does). In fact, this historical location is thought of collectively as the symbol of the definitive fall of royal absolutism.

The Bastille was constructed between 1370 and 1383; the impressive citadel was a vast rectangle measuring 216 feet by 98 feet, with 8 towers 78 feet high and surrounded by an 82 foot wide moat. It became the state prison during the reign of Louis XIII, and prisoners were simply put away by *lettre de cachet*, that is, by the king's order.

The prison housed illustrious characters such as the Duc de Nemours, Voltaire, the Marquis de Sade, Mirabeau and the Man in the Iron Mask. However, they did not suffer much, as they could take their servants and furniture with them and receive visitors.

On July 14, 1789, the Parisian people, armed with weapons, stormed the Bastille. The date marks the overthrow of the Old Regime. A businessman named Palloy ordered the demolition of the fortress and sent small models of the Bastille cut from the stones that had once belonged to the building to all the villages in France. A railway station was built on the site in 1859; by 1970, it was no longer in use and was demolished in 1984. The new opera house, built by Carlos Ott, now stands in its place.

The architect was chosen from among hundreds of candidates in a competition that was judged on November 17, 1983. The construction works began a year later, and the Opera was inaugurated in July 1989, marking the bicentenary of the French Revolution. It is remarkable mainly for its vast dimensions: the floor area measures 164,042 square feet, the building rises 157 feet from the ground, has a huge main hall that can seat 2,700 persons, an amphitheatre for 600, a multi-purpose hall, enormous areas backs stage, scenery workshops, storage areas, reception halls (one of which is as large as the main stage) and other underground premises, built 66 feet below street-level.

It is impossible to remain indifferent to the building's exterior architecture. The shapes (semi-cylinders and parallelepipeds), the proportions and the materials, all skilfully chosen by Carlos Ott, create a homogenous whole. On the interior, the original design (combining curves and straight lines) and the sober decor of contrasting light and dark shades achieves an elegant harmony.

The colors and shapes are austere, given that Carlos Ott believed the real scenery should be on the stage. Ergonomics were studied very closely, to create perfect acoustics.

Rue du Faubourg-Saint-Antoine is located to the east of the Place de la Bastille; it has been the fief of fine furniture craftsmen since the Middle Ages.

Boulle, the most famous cabinetmaker, was lucky enough to attract Louis XIV's attention, which led Colbert to authorize the royal studios to manufacture and sell their models. Towards the northeast lies Rue de la Roquette. This quarter, once a densely populated area, has become "trendy" since the 1980s.

The street ends at Boulevard de Ménilmontant and the Père-Lachaise cemetery. Towards the north, Boulevard Beaumarchais crosses the wide Haussmannian boulevards.

The square

The first stone was laid in 1370 by the provost of Paris, Hugues Aubriot. The monument known as the walled town of Saint-Antoine, was the most dreaded of all fortresses for four centuries. One of the most famous "residents," Latude, was locked in for thirty-five years, but was finally freed: Sacha Guitry recalled his many escapes in the film "Si Paris nous était conté." On July 14, 1789, the people of Paris, revolted against this symbol of royal power and broke down the doors. Revolutionaries are especially fond of the place. The column that stands there today was erected to commemorate those who fell during the fighting in July 1830. The statue of the Génie de la Bastille was restored for the bicentenary of the Revolution. The square still has a popular aura, even in our time. On the night of the elections in 1981, the Socialists decided to celebrate their victory here. On the right, the Opera House that replaced the Palais Garnier – now reserved for ballet – opened in 1989.

The Marais

In prehistoric times, the Seine spread out freely to the foot of the hills on the right bank, and left a marshy area when it moved back to its current riverbed. The Romans built a road between Lutetia and Melun over the marshes. The houses on Rue Saint-Antoine were built along this road. During the 13th century, monks cleared the marshes and started to use them as agricultural land. The name of the Rue des Coutures-Saint-Gervais recalls this period. From Rue des Francs-Bourgeois to the Quai des Célestins, the quarter was surrounded by Philippe Auguste's city walls (about 1190), and the king encouraged the construction of houses inside the newly created town walls.

During the 14th century, Charles V erected a new wall all the way to the Bastille area. He ordered the construction of the Hôtel Saint-Paul in 1361, when he no longer wished to remain in the palace of the Cité with its dreadful memories. The *hôtel* was finished in 1365, and stood in between Rue Saint-Antoine, Rue Saint-Paul, Rue du Petit-Musc (then known as Pute-y-Muse, or "the whore who strolls here") and the Quai des Célestins. Charles VI went mad after the tragic festivities of the Bal des Ardents in 1393 when five young lords covered themselves with tar to resemble savages, and were scorched to death when their bodies caught fire from the torches. The king was saved by the Duchesse de Berry who wrapped her dress around him. He died here much later in 1422. Charles VII and his successors preferred the Hôtel des Tournelles residence. Francis I finally sold it in 1543. It was then destroyed and divided into plots. The only traces of Hôtel Saint-Paul are the names of the surrounding streets: Rue Charles V, Rue Beautreillis (recalling the garden vines) and Rue des Lions (evoking the royal menagerie).

Hôtels particuliers

The 17th century was the heyday for building *hôtels particuliers* in the Marais district. At the end of the century, the quarter was somewhat abandoned in favor of the Île Saint-Louis, and then it fell into total neglect when the nobility decided to move towards the west, and settle on the road to Versailles. The Faubourgs of Saint-Germain and Saint-Honoré replaced the old Marais, whose medieval streets had begun to look unfit for habitation.

It remained a center for craftsmen and merchants, who installed their workshops all around the mansions. The area became increasingly dilapidated until the recent renovation of the Marais, promoted by the Malraux law.

The Hôtel de Sully was built for a banker by Jean Androuet du Cerceau around 1630. Sully bought it in 1634 and embellished it with statues of the four elements and the seasons, which can be seen in the courtyard. He ordered the construction of the small Sully residence behind it, which is linked to the Place des Vosges at number 7 bis. Here, in 1725, Voltaire was beaten up by the Chevalier de Rohan's valets. When he demanded redress, he was sent to the Bastille prison and later went into exile in England.

The Saint-Paul-Saint-Louis church recalls the Jesuits' revenge on the Jansenists. Under Richelieu's protection, the Jesuits built a typical Jesuit church modeled on the Gésu church in Rome. Richelieu celebrated the first mass in 1641 and Fléchier, Bourdaloue and Bossuet displayed their oratorical talents. It was a very fashionable church until 1763, when the Jesuits were again blacklisted. The church was ransacked under the Revolution, and in 1802 became a simple parish church in an area that had lost its brilliance.

The Hôtel de Sens (like the Hôtel de Cluny) is a typical example of the private mansions built in the Middle Ages, though it was not completed until 1507. The façade has two oblique turrets and a third facing Rue de l'Hôtel-de-Ville. Two gargoyles have been reconstructed and the hall features a vault in the flamboyant Gothic style. The building's square tower makes it look like a fortress.

It belonged to the archbishops of Sens who were in charge of the Diocese of Paris until 1622 and became one of the headquarters of the ultra-Catholic League during the wars of religion. Queen Margot once lived here. Todays it houses the Forney decorative arts library.

Hôtel de Carnavalet

A statue of Louis XIV sculpted by Coysevox currently decorates the courtyard of the Paris Historical Museum, now annexed to the neighboring hôtel, Le Peletier-de-Saint-Fargeau. The residence is decorated with casement windows, sculptures by Jean Goujon, Renaissance and Mansart façades. It was used by Madame de Sévigné, and was considerably enlarged in the 19th century when it was turned into a museum. Visitors can follow the evolution of the city through a large collection of paintings as well as interior and exterior decorative elements from places that no longer exist. Everything on display here, including panelling from the Colbert residence and from the Military Café located on Rue Saint-Honoré, furniture, signs, trompe l'œil decorations created by Boucher for a shop in the île de la Cite, as well as souvenirs of the Marquise de Sévigné, has been chosen to give visitors an idea of what Paris looked like over the centuries.

The Hôtel de Carnavalet was built in 1544 and remodeled in 1661 by Mansart. Its name comes from the deformation of the name of a previous owner: Madame de Kernevoy. Madame de Sévigné lived here from 1677 to 1696.

In 1880, it became the Paris Historical Museum and was enlarged to include the Hôtel Le Peletier de Saint-Fargeau (17th century) and was recently remodeled. The museum's collections of paintings, engravings, furniture and models reconstruct everyday life in Paris over the centuries.

The Hôtel de Lamoignon (Rue Pavée), named after a president of Parliament, was built in 1584 for Diane de France, a legitimized daughter of Henry III. It is currently the seat of the Paris Historical Library. Its Corinthian columns are the oldest in Paris.

The Hôtel de Marle (Rue Payenne) now houses the Swedish Cultural Center.

There are many interesting *hôtels particuliers* on Rue des Francs-Bourgeois (which was named in about 1330 for the inhabitants of a "charity house" who were too poor to pay taxes) such as Hôtel de Sandreville (no. 26), Hôtel de Barbes (no.33), and Hôtel de Coulanges (no.35). The Kwok-On Museum (no.41), named after the donor, houses an Asian theater.

One of the towers from the Philippe Auguste walls is located at no.55, inside the courtyard of the Credit Municipal Bank.

The church of Notre-Dame-des-Blancs-Manteaux was named after the white habit worn by mendicant monks in the time of Saint-Louis. It was reconstructed in 1685 and is renowned for its organ concerts.

The Hôtel Salé (1658) was built for a salt tax collector and named after the tax. It attracts many tourists between Beaubourg and the Place des Vosges, as it is now the Picasso Museum. Several hundred paintings and sculptures and many drawings by the artist are displayed here.

The Hôtel Libéral-Bruant (rue de la Perle) dates back to 1685 and currently houses the Bricard de la Serrure Museum. The Hotel Guénégaud (Rue des Archives) was designed by Mansart (1651) and has since become the museum of Hunting and Nature. Opposite no.47 of the rue Vielle-du-TempleDuc Louis d'Orléans was murdered by the henchmen of Jean the Fearless in 1407. The mansion built in 1655 became the residence of the Dutch Ambassadors. Beaumarchais wrote *The Marriage of Figaro* here. The *hôtel* has a beautiful door and a splendid courtyard.

The two corbelled turrets and the door at no.58 Rue des Archives are the only vestiges of the medieval manor house that Oliver de Clisson, du Guesclin's partner, built in 1375. The Duc de Guise planned the Saint-Barthélemy massacre here.

In 1704, the architect Delamair started to build a residence for the Princesse de Soubise (a mistress of Louis XIV) on the site. He kept the door made by Clisson and created a horseshoe-shaped classical main courtyard surrounded by a gallery of paired columns and pilasters. Delamair also designed Cardinal de Rohan's neighbouring residence.

The décor of the Hôtel de Soubise, the last *hôtel particulier* to be built in the Marais (18th century), was completed by Boffrand. It is the only one that can be visited today that still has its original decorations. It now houses the Museum of French History.

In 1808, the Hôtel de Soubise became the seat of the National Archives. In order to store the country's document collection (now numbering several billion), it has spread to the neighboring Hôtels de Rohan, d'Assy, de Jancourt and le Tonnelier de Breteuil.

The Hôtel de Beauvais, Rue François-Miron, was built for Anne of Austria's chambermaid, Cateau la Borgnesse, who made her fortune by "sexually initiating" young Louis XIV, who was only sixteen years old. Anne of Austria, Henrietta of France (Queen of England) and her daughter, Henrietta of England, watched the wedding of Louis XIV and Marie-Thérèse from the balcony of the residence. Mozart and his family stayed here in 1763; a medallion recalls the moment in the magnificent semi-oval courtyard.

The Hôtel d'Aumont built was built in the 17th century by the poet Scarron's uncle, who was Madame de Maintenon's first husband. It currently houses the Administrative Court of the Seine Department. On Rue des Rosiers, Hebrew inscriptions on kosher shops, bakeries and bookshops preserve the traditional, timeless atmosphere of the city's old Jewish quarter.

The Hôtel de Soubise

The Princesse de Soubise gave Louis XIV two children. With each birth, her cooperative husband increased his fortune, until he was rich enough to build one of the most prestigious residences in the Marais. Classical style façades hide refined decorations that were added during the reign of Louis XV by painters and architects from Versailles. As the mansion had been abandoned for a while, Napoleon decided to use it for the national archives. The archives are now being reorganized and some documents are currently housed in the neighboring Hôtel de Rohan and a new building, on Rue des Quatre-Fils. Visitors as well as historians and researchers can come and see documents such as the Carolingian decrees, a letter written by Joan of Arc and Colbert's manuscripts.

Place des Vosges

The Hôtel des Tournelles became a royal residence in 1407. Charles IV came occasionally and the Duke of Bedford resided here during the English occupation. Charles VII, Louis XI, Charles VIII, Louis XII, Francis I and Henri II all lived here at some point. The latter died here in 1559 after being wounded by Montgomery, the captain of his Scottish guards, in a tournament held in Rue Saint-Antoine.

The residence and gardens spread out between the Rue des Tournelles, Rue de Turenne and Rue Saint-Antoine, on grounds that were much larger than today's Place des Vosges. Catherine de Medecis had the house torn down in 1563, and a horse market was opened here. In 1578, a duel was fought between three of Henry III's "mignons" and three partisans of Henri de Guise.

Paris did not have a proper square to hold public celebrations or simply for promenades. Henry IV wanted a Royal Square. The superb complex built in this square has hardly changed over the years. There are still 36 townhouses (nine on each side) with four arcades per townhouse (except nos. 1 and 28 which have only three), and four tall windows on each floor.

Henry IV was murdered in 1610, and never saw his royal square completed. It was inaugurated in 1612 after the double marriage of Louis XIII with Anne of Austria and her sister Elizabeth of France with the future Philippe IV of Spain. A great celebration was held here, where 10,000 spectators were treated to an equestrian ballet with 1,300 horsemen performing to music played by 150 musicians.

Duels continued to be fought until Richelieu banned them by a royal edict. The Comte de Montmorency-Bouteville broke the law and was decapitated at the Place de Grève in 1627. Tallemant des Réaux recounts how a close friend of the Duc de Candalle promised a soldier a golden shield if he dared "to bed his tart in the middle of Place Royale". He carried out the dare, providing "a fine spectacle that was watched by all the ladies from their windows." An edict issued in 1656 forbade wanton women to stroll under the arches. People played for high stakes at Blondeau's gambling den.

Between 1610 and 1660, the townhouses in Place Royale were sought after by aristocrats and financiers. It was known simply as "La Place" (the Square). During the Revolution, its named was changed to Place des Fédérés and then to Place de l'Indivisibilité. It was levelled out to be used as a parade ground by the National Guard and workshops were set up to manufacture weapons. In 1800, under Napoleon Bonaparte's first Consulate, the square was named "Place des Vosges" in honour of the first French department to pay all its taxes. The current gate was built in 1839, after the first one, built by contributions from townhouse owners during the reign of Louis XIV, was destroyed during the reign of Louis-Philippe. The statue

**The façades
of the Place des Vosges**

On the site of the Hotel de Tournelles, Henry IV ordered the construction of a closed square like those built during the Middle Ages, surrounded by townhouses of red brick and white stone. Each one had two main floors, and a ground floor decorated with an elegant gallery of archways, to protect pedestrians from bad weather. Today, nearly four centuries later, the façades are as much admired as they were when the square was inaugurated.

of Louis XIII was sculpted in 1819; its predecessor, donated by Richelieu, was melted down during the Revolution.

No king ever lived in the King's House, located at no. 1, where the arches open out onto Rue de Birague and the roof dominates the square. Marie de Rabutin-Chantal, the future Marquise de Sévigné, was born at no. 1 bis in 1626. Two *precieuses*, former ladies-in-waiting of Marie de Medicis, lived at no. 5. One of them, Madeleine de Souvré, was the mistress of the duellist Montmorency-Bouteville and the poet Voiture. During the 17th century,

the Duc de Chaulnes owned no. 9 and the famous actress Rachel resided there in 1856. Marion Delorme, who lived at no. 11, counted the poet des Barreaux, Cinq-Mars and Cardinal Richelieu among her numerous lovers. When the Marquise de Piennes lived at no. 4 in 1636, her literary salon was particularly favored by the *precieuses*. The Marquis de Favras lived there before being hanged in 1790 for plotting to kidnap Louis XVI and assassinate Bailly, La Fayette and Necker. The symmetrical Queen's House, opposite the King's, is located at no. 28. It also opens out to the exterior and bears a medallion decorated

Hôtel de Ville

The Hôtel de Ville or town hall is considered the true center of popular power, and during every trooubled period in French history, success has depended on who succeeded in conquering it. For example, in August 1944, it became the main headquarters of the Resistance in the fight against the occupying troops.

Until 1830, the square on which the Hôtel de Ville is located, was known as the Place de Grève.

During the Old Regime, it was used for public executions. Unemployed men and, later, discontented workers, used to meet here in protest, whence the name *greve* which means "strike".

During the 12th century, the water transport guilds turned the adjacent port into one of the largest in Paris. A century later, Saint-Louis appointed a Provost from among the local merchants, assisted by aldermen, to take charge

Hôtel de Ville

The origin of its construction dates from the royal visit by Mary of England to Paris where she was to marry Louis II in 1514. The Pillared House, set up by Etienne Marcel in the Place de Grève for the merchants' Provost, was too small to accommodate the crowd, so François I entrusted Bocador with the plans for a new town hall The Hapsburgs, the most influential rulers at the time, had magnificent town halls in the center of the cities under their rule in Spain and the Netherlands. Paris did not wish to be outdone. The Place de Grève, which extends to the Seine, was the scene of many Parisian celebrations and political events. On July 17, 1789, Bailly, the mayor of Paris, presented a tricolor cockade to Louis XVI: red and blue represented the city, and white the royalty, which La Fayette demanded to have included in the colors of the French flag. On July 27, 1794, Robespierre sought refuge in the building, but was arrested and sent to the guillotine the following day. The Hôtel de Ville was burnt down during the Commune and was entirely rebuilt between 1872 and 1882 by Ballu and Deperthes, who tried to make it resemble as closely as possible the original under François I.

of municipal administration. They met in a common house near the Abbey of Sainte-Geneviève. In 1357, Etienne Marcel, a wealthy draper and Provost at the time, forced the Royal Council to include representatives of the Estates General. That same year, he bought the Pillared House, located in the Place de Grève, to serve as the city's first Hôtel de Ville. The square was considerably enlarged in the 18th century, and then again by Haussmann. Since then, it has been the scene of both riots and festivities. In 1382, the Maillotins revolted here against income taxes. The rebels pillaged the Châtelet, grabbed lead mallets they found in the Hôtel de Ville and pursued the tax collectors.

During the July Revolution, the square was taken over by 50,000 people who clashed with the royal guards. Louis-Philippe was proclaimed king of France, but was in turn ousted by the Revolution of 1848. On February 24, a provisional government was set up at the Hôtel de Ville, and the following day, Lamartine read a speech that is still renowned today, in which he refused the red flag used by the revolutionaries and insisted on keeping the tricolour flag. On September 24, 1870, Léon Gambetta, Jules Favre and Jules Ferry proclaimed the Republic. During the Prussian siege of Paris, the people of Paris invaded the Hôtel de Ville to reject the armistice and proclaim the Commune.

However, the history of the Hôtel de Ville is not just a string of riots and executions. Many magnificent receptions and popular celebrations have been held here.

Châtelet

A curious vestige called the Tour de Saint-Jacques is located a bit farther up the Rue de Rivoli. The Gothic bell-tower is the only remaining part of what was once the Church of Saint-Jacques-la-Boucherie, built in the 11th century, altered in the 16th century and torn down during the Empire. It was the departure point for pilgrims on the route to Santiago de Compostela. Pascal carried out experiments on the weight of air here. If the bell tower is still standing, it is thanks to a gunsmith who bought it in 1797. Molten lead ran down from the top of the tower into water tubs, where it solidified into a perfect sphere.

For a long time, the name "Châtelet" was synonymous with "prison." The 12th century fortress known as the Grand Châtelet (opposite the Petit Châtelet which stood on the Left Bank until 1782) remained on the site until 1802. Its dungeons bore dreadful names such as "the Barbarity" and "the Pit," and were occupied by many famous prisoners such as the poets Villon and Clément Marot.

The square was developed during the Empire period, and Davioud built two theatres in 1860. The first was the Théâtre du Châtelet, which became the Théâtre Musical de Paris in 1980; the second, which faces it, is the Théâtre de la Ville, was once known as the Théâtre Sarah Bernhardt.

Les Halles

The Forum

In 1335, when the Paris market had become too small to serve the city's needs, King Louis VI, known as Louis the Fat, ordered it to be moved from the Place de Grève to a place called "Les Champeaux". Philippe Auguste and Saint Louis enlarged the area, and from then on, the new buildings were known as "Les Halles".

Les Halles again proved too small under the reign of François I, and his son, Henri II, ordered a new market to be built in 1553 reserved for selling food. The wheat market was added on in 1765, and the market of Les Innocents in 1788.

Napoleon III had Baltard design ten pavilions, remarkable examples of iron and glass architecture, which were built between 1854 and 1866. The buildings were not well received, with the mildest criticism describing them as "umbrellas of glass and metal."

The quarter has always been a center of trade. In 1963, the council decided to remodel the area, and in 1969, the Parisian wholesale food market was moved to Rungis, six and a half miles south of the capital, and the pavilions were demolished. The names of the streets, such as Rue du Lard (Bacon), Rue de la Poterie (Pottery), Rue de la Lingerie, and so on, recall the guilds and craftsmen that were once established here.

Emile Zola's book *The Belly of Paris* takes us back to the days when Baltard's pavilions were still in place. The author presents a perfect description of the lively quarter, with fruit and vegetables piled up on the pavement near the fresh, still bloody meat. The biggest wholesalers and retailers kept their stock in the recesses of old courtyards or in deep cellars, and their food stands spilled out onto the sidewalks. Late-night revellers would come to end the evening sipping onion soup or nibbling oysters alongside crate carriers, while butchers in bloodstained smocks got their strength back with a drink at the noisy bars.

After Baltard's constructions were torn down, all that was left was a large hole, which remained there for several years, as nobody quite knew how it should be filled.

Finally, the decision was made to design an area to be used especially by young people. At the same time,

Pages 68-69:
**The Forum
of Les Halles**

The Forum was a large square, copied from the Greek agora, where the Romans met to discuss state affairs. Nowadays this is a pedestrian area where people can walk around freely The remodelling of the excavations of Les Halles created a pleasant modern space and opened up an area surrounded by constructions from different eras. The church of Saint-Eustache, famous for its organ, is located to the right, and in the distance, the Rotunda of the Bourse de Commerce where there once stood a convent, a palace, a gambling den and a wheat market.

the residents of the neighborhood wanted a project in keeping with the architecture of the past. It also became clear that a rapid transit system was needed and the hole of Les Halles would have to serve as a railway junction. The result was the Châtelet-Les Halles Métro station, which is the largest in Europe.

The Forum, an underground village with streets, avenues, shops, restaurants and cinemas, was inaugurated in 1979. Vasconi and Penchréach designed the large shopping center, which has five floors bathed in light, even though four of them are below street level.

The Forum constantly draws a huge number of people. It offers numerous attractions, including Saint-Eustache Square, the Discotheque de France, a swimming pool and the Paris video library which were all opened in 1986. Parisians and tourists alike can enjoy leisure and cultural activities and a shopping complex in the center of Paris, in an area tha has changed the face of the French capital.

Towering above the entire complex stands the old church of Saint-Eustache, where Jean-Baptiste Poquelin (better known as Molière) was baptized in 1622.

Beaubourg
(Georges Pompidou Center)

In 1969, President Georges Pompidou was thinking about creating a large cultural area in the center of Paris to display contemporary art work in all of its myriad shapes and forms.

By the end of 1970, an international invitation to tender was announced, and in 1971, the project presented by Renzo Piano and Richard Rogers was selected. They built the Beaubourg center, which was inaugurated on January 31, 1977, an event that made the headlines worldwide. The architecture is still very controversial. Its iron beams, glass and multicoloured plastic have met with admiration as well as criticsm. Alongside the library and the museum with its wealth of contemporary art, temporary exhibitions, discussions, films and dance events attract an ever-increasing number of visitors whose interest has created a snowball effect in art galleries and in the publishing world.

The façade
of the Beaubourg centre

11ᵗʰ century etymology refers to "Beau bourg". However, the centre of Paris has nothing left of that rustic area. Not everyone supported the architects' decision to voluntarily exhibit functional elements (especially the pipes) on the outside of the façade of the cultural center, thus freeing the maximum amount of interior space. Nonetheless, it was Beaubourg that restored the intellectual and artistic renown of Paris.

The area surrounding
the Forum

The demolition of the market at Les Halles left a large open space that has not been completely taken up by the Forum. Modern buildings, some of them featuring glass façades, stand next to renovated constructions.

Place des Victoires

Place des Victoires, located close to the Forum, is the city's fashion center, situated between the grandiose head office of the Banque de France, Rue de la Vrillière and Notre-Dame-des-Victoires Basilica, and Place des Petits-Pères, created by Louis XIII after the victory of La Rochelle. Usually, the authorities have the problem of deciding on which monument should be erected in a new square. Here, the normal process was reversed and the square, built at the same time as Place Vendôme, was created to display a statue.

Maréchal de La Feuillade commissioned the equestrian statue of Louis XIV designed by Jules Hardouin-Mansart, and he joined forces with the City of Paris to create a setting worthy of the Sun King. It was a clever gift, and the sovereign acknowledged the work with 120,000 pounds. Even so, La Feuillade ended up bankrupt.

Saint-Eustache

A chapel was built in the center of Les Halles in the 13th century. Until that time, Saint-Germain-l'Auxerrois had served as the neighborhood church, but it had become too small for the population growth resulting from the proximity of the Louvre palace and busy Rue Saint-Honoré. The small chapel was transformed into a new church, which in turn became too small and was rebuilt in the 14th century. Although construction work began under François I, the church was not completed until a century later, during the reign of Louis XIII. The large building combines Gothic and Renaissance architecture, and was surrounded by merchants' stalls during the Middle Ages, until Baltard's Halles were built. Nowadays, the silhouette of Saint-Eustache watches over a different style of trade: the Forum shopping center. Colbert is buried in the church and a modernist sculpture by Henri de Miller is located in the church square, inviting passers-by to pause for a moment with a single word: "Ecoute" (Listen).

Palais-Royal

The palace

In 1624, Cardinal Richelieu built himself a sumptuous residence, known as "Cardinal Palace", which was designed by Jacques Lemercier. To silence his critics, Richelieu announced in 1636 that he would bequeathe the palace to the King. Thus, Louis XIII became the owner when the minister died in 1643, and afterwards Anne of Austria resided here with young Louis XIV. The Regent Queen preferred this mansion to the Louvre, and Mazarin moved here as well, after residing at the nearby Hôtel Tubuef, on the Rue Neuve-des-Petits-Champs. In 1661, the palace was attributed to Philippe d'Orléans, the brother of Louis XIV. Philippe's son became Regent when the Sun King died in 1715, and gave parties here that earned him the reputation of a libertine lord.

The building was rebuilt after a fire in 1763, and given the appearance it has today. The Regent's great-grandson, Duc Louis-Philippe d'Orleans, who was heavily in debt, decided to engage in real estate speculation and surrounded the Palais-Royal gardens with housing. The ground floors of the buildings were to be taken up by galleries and shops. Victor Louis built sixty townhouses with groundfloor archways between 1781 and 1784. He also remodelled the palace.

The area attracted noblemen, bourgeois, artists along with the lower classes. Chamfort described it as the "Parisian people's forum". The police were not allowed to enter this royal domain, and hence it became a place where people enjoyed freedom of thought and behaved as they wished. On July 13, 1789, Camille Desmoulins stood on a table at the Café de Foy and mobilized the crowd with the first call to arms of the Revolution. The crowd used chestnut leaves as cockades. Noble titles were abolished in 1792. Philippe d'Orleans became Philippe-Egalité, and the Royal Palace became the Palais-Egalité (Equality Palace).

Gaming rooms were quite common here during the Empire and the Restoration, until Louis-Philippe shut them down in 1836. Thereafter, Palais-Royal became a quieter area. The building was partly burnt down during the revolutions in 1848 and 1871, and Chabrol completed its reconstruction in 1876.

The gardens

The gardens of Palais-Royal, where nothing changes except the seasons, are a haven of tranquility amid the bustle of Paris. In the springtime, blossoms and green grass give the gardens the aura of a sweet-smelling oasis, clearly distinct from the density of stone buildings surrounding it. Yet, unlike pedestrian squares such as the Piazza Navona in Rome or the Plaza Mayor in Madrid or Salamanca, the gardens of Palais-Royal have retained a quaint charm, without any cafés or tourists, frequented only by garden-lovers and habitués. The calm is all the more unusual in that the famous Buren columns and Poly Bury's metal fountains lie just beyond the Restoration-style double colonnade known as the Galérie d'Orléans. A few steps away, opposite the façade of the Palais-Royal, on the other side of Rue de Rivoli, stands the entrance to the Louvre, with its Pyramid and thousands of tourists. Palais-Royal has been the seat of the French Conseil d'Etat since 1875, and houses the Conseil Constitutional in the Montpensier wing and the Ministry of Culture in the Valois wing.

The Comédie-Française

Nowadays, when people think of the Comédie-Française, they think of Molière. In fact, however, the author never presented a play in this marvellous theater, as it was not built until the end of the 18th century. The building was designed by Victor Louis. The name "Comédie-Française" dates back to 1680, whereas Molière had already been dead seven years, while playing the title role of *Le Malade Imaginaire*.

Molière created his Illustre Théâtre in 1643. Until then, his company had spent years searching for audiences in the provinces. When he returned to Paris in 1658, Molière found himself performing before Monsieur, the King's brother, who was charmed. He was then invited to perform for the King, and when his play made Louis XIV laugh, it was clear he held a winning

hand. Molière's company performed at Versailles and Palais-Royal, and the King protected his troupe from the opposition of the clergy. Louis XIV was not yet under the influence of Madame de Maintenon, who was fiercely opposed to theater and considered it harmful.

Thus, on August 25, 1680, hearts beat wildly on stage. Three theater companies had joined together for the first time: the troupes from the Hôtel de Bourgogne, Les Italiens and Molière's Illustre Théâtre. The King had decided to order the rival companies to form a single troupe and a *lettre de cachet* made their existence official. A century later, tempers flared, and the Revolution split the group into royalists and republicans, neither of whom concealed their opinions. Talma led the republicans to the Odéon Theater, where the troupe performed in Victor Louis Hall. A few years later, the company reunited and has continued performing in this location ever since. Napoleon, like Louis XIV before him, was very interested

in the organisation of the company, and in 1812, he issued a decree from Moscow granting a unique status to the Comédie-Française, with shareholding members and salaried actors and an administrator chosen by the authorities. This status has hardly changed since then.

On February 25, 1830, the Comédie-Française was once again in the Paris limelight. At the opening of *Hernani*, long-haired young men wearing red vests – the Romantics – asserted their belief in new theater. Led by Victor Hugo, they opposed the Classics and made fun of their wigs. Wild fighting ensured between the groups.

Since then, the Comédie-Française has presented a wide variety of classic and modern plays as well as those by foreign authors. Until recent times, the public went to the theater, not for the plays, but to see the actors, including Talma, Mademoiselle Mars, Mounet-Sully, Sarah Bernhardt, Béatrix Dussane, Louis Seigner, Jacques Charron, Pierre Dux, Robert Hirsch, etc.

The Louvre

The Louvre, which has been a "work-in-progress" every since the initial dungeon built by Philippe Auguste, is now the largest palace in the world.

The origin of the construction dates back to the end of the 12th century, when Philippe Auguste wished to fortify the city before he left on the crusades. Paris was surrounded by ramparts reinforced by towers along the Seine, including one at the Louvre. The original Louvre was a small fortress built around a tower and surrounded by a moat. Philippe Auguste assembled the country's archives here, Saint-Louis added a chapel and Philippe the Fair made it the seat of the Treasury and an arsenal.

Paris extended its terrain considerably during the 15th century, and Charles V ordered the construction of new walls. The Louvre was now in the center of the city and no longer played a strategic role, prompting the king to turn the useless fortress into a place of enjoyment, adorned with statues and housing the first royal art collections along with a library filled with manuscripts.

Charles deserved to be called "the Wise", as his library contained almost a thousand volumes, including Saint-Louis' Psalter and the *Roman de la Rose*. Charles V liked to surround himself with men and women of letters, such as Christine de Pisan, amid the refined décor of heavy wall-hangings and painted beams. After his reign, however, the Louvre was abandoned for over a century in favor of the castles in the Loire Valley and the Hôtel Saint-Paul.

François I, who was defeated at Pavia in 1525 and taken prisoner for a year, was released against a ransom paid by the people of Paris. He decided to live at Louvre, but it was in such a dilapidated state that it first had to be restored and modernized.

In the eyes of the Renaissance king, the Louvre resembled a cramped, decayed mansion when compared to the new castles built on the banks of the Loire. François I had the central tower demolished, the moat filled in and a large wharf created on the Seine, the present Quai du Louvre. Though the "Father of Letters" died shortly after the beginning of the construction works, he gave the impetus for the process leading up to the modern day Louvre. He put Pierre Lescot in charge of a total renovation in 1546. The architect worked on

The Pyramid and the Napoleon Courtyard

The pyramid was built as part of a remodelling plan known as the Grand Louvre project. For over a century, much of the Louvre had been taken up by the Ministry of Finance, which was finally moved to Bercy. As a result, the entire palace was freed for museum display, and the treasures that had lain dormant in the storage areas of "Louvre City," as Nicolas Philibert called it, could finally be displayed. The project to modernize the building also involved clearing the underground areas dating back to the time of Philippe Auguste and Charles V. Exhibits are on view to show the development of the palace over the centuries. An auditorium, a book shop and a documentation center have been added to the many art collections visited every year by over four million people.

the building for thirty-two years, through five different reigns. He used the former building foundations and added the West and South wings, consisting of a ground floor, an upper floor and an attic. The façades were generously decorated with fluted columns, pilasters, niches with statues and remarkable friezes designed by the architect and sculptor Jean Goujon. When Pierre Lescot died, he had completed only two wings, and until the 18th century, the building had two Renaissance-style wings and two others, the East and North, in Gothic style. Despite the sketchy condition of his palace, François I had started collecting art works brought back from Italy. One of them was the Mona Lisa.

In 1563, Catherine de Medicis found the palace too small and engaged Philibert Delorme to build a new castle called the Tuileries Palace. She devised a covered gallery extending along the Seine called the Galerie du Bord de l'Eau (Waterside Gallery), connecting the two palaces, but the construction was halted during the wars of religion.

When Henry IV took possession of his kingdom, he started the works again. He continued the Gallery and added the Pavilion de Flore, designed by Jacques II Androuet du Cerceau. Henri IV, called the "Builder King," had many artists and craftsmen come and work in the gallery, which became a genuine art center.

Under the reign of Louis XIII, Le Mercier built the Clock Pavilion and continued the construction of the Cour Carrée (Square Courtyard) under the reign of Louis XIII. The area of the palace should have been increased fourfold, but when the king died, Anne of Austria moved to the Cardinal Palace and the works were abandoned once again.

Sixteen years later, in 1659, Louis XIV resumed the project. When the Fronde uprisings ended, the sovereign returned to the Louvre, followed by Mazarin and his large family. The Gothic-style areas along with the *hôtel particuliers* built around the royal residence were razed and rebuilt by Le Vau in harmony with more recent additions.

Pages 76-77:
The Cour Carrée

The harmonious façades of the Cour Carrée or Square Courtyard were built under the reigns of François I, Louis XIII and Louis XIV by a series of talented architects. The dungeon of the original fortress was discovered in this courtyard. The medieval palace of Charles V, which was surrounded by towers, occupied only part of the current courtyard, which was extended to the west by the sovereigns that succeeded him.

The Pont des Arts

A classical façade, closing off the Cour Carrée on side of the Seine, was built under Louis XIV at the same time as the colonnade opposite Saint-Germain-l'Auxerrois. During the Empire, an iron bridge (later rebuilt using steel) was constructed when the Academy of Fine Arts was established. The footbridge leads to the French Institute on the Left Bank. From the bridge, one has a splendid view of the Galerie du Bord de l'Eau (Waterside Gallery) to the left of the section shown here, the Ile de la Cité with its skyline of towers and spires, and a long vista along both sides of the river.

Molière made his debut before the King in the Hall of the Cariatides, an architectural masterpiece by Goujon.

Louis XIV wanted a grandiose eastern façade opposite the Saint-Germain-l'Auxerrois church. Bernini proposed such far-reaching transformations that the King refused, despite his own penchant for construction work. Instead, he chose the more modest project presented by Le Vau, Le Brun and Claude Perrault which, cuilminated in the construction of a classical colonnade. The façade was not completed, as the Sun King and his court moved to Versailles in 1682. The Louvre was abandoned and in the difficult years that ensued, it was occupied by a series of curious tenants. First, the arts academies were set up there. Le Brun opened the "Cabinet of the King's Paintings" (containing 2,500 works) to the public, and starting in1699, the Grand Gallery housed an exhibition of paintings and sculpture. The artists were soon joined by a cohort of parasites. Sheds were put up in the Cour Carrée and cabarets and boatmen added to the general chaos. The buildings were in such a sorry state that by

the middle of the 18th century, they were slated for destruction. The Louvre was saved by Marigny, the brother of the King's mistress, Madame de Pompadour. He opposed demolition and drove out the various building occupants. Gabriel and Soufflot cleared out the colonnade and restored it.

In 1793, the Convention transformed the Louvre into a "Museum of the Republic". Napoleon enriched its collections by ordering defeated countries to pay tribute in the form of art works. Percier and Fontaine finished the Cour Carrée and the colonnade, and erected a triumphal arch in the Carrousel gardens to mark the victories of 1805. The Emperor married Marie-Louise in the Cour Carrée on April 1, 1810.

Under Napoleon III, Lefuel and Visconti realized the long-cherished dream of joining the two castles completely by means of the Rivoli gallery. Not long afterwards, in 1871, the Tuileries palace was burnt down, in 1871, and finally razed in 1883. Since then, the Louvre has looked essentially the same, opening onto the Tuileries

Gardens, in line with the obelisk and the Triumphal Arch.

The glass pyramid in front of the Clock Pavilion, designed by the architect I.M. Pei, became the new public entrance to the museum in March 1989.

The various museum departments display many masterpieces in addition to the Mona Lisa. Roman, Greek and Egyptian statuary includes the *Venus de Milo*, the *Winged Victory of Samothrace* and the *Seated Scribe*. Among the foreign sculpture is featured Michaelangelo's *Slaves*, and there are works of Flemish, Spanish, English and Italian painters (Vermeer, El Greco, Gainsborough, Titian, Tintoretto, etc.), as well as French masters (Watteau, Fragonard, Ingres, etc.), up to the beginning of Impressionism painting, which is exhibited at the Orsay Museum.

The church of Saint-Germain-l'Auxerrois is located opposite the colonnade, and presents an odd silhouette due to the vagaries of its construction. This place of worship has been in use since the 6th century, and has been remodelled on so many occasions that it has a Romanesque steeple, a Gothic choir and central portal, a Flamboyant Gothic porch, nave, and transept and a Renaissance portal. The church was restored during the 19th century following heavy damage during the Revolution. For centuries, it was the parish church of the kings of France and their entourage.

The National Library and the Bourse

In 1721, the Mazarin Palace was chosen as the official seat of the National Library, which had been located previously in smaller premises on Rue Vivienne. The library contains coins and treasures from the medal cabinet, illuminated manuscripts from the Middle Ages as well as contemporary ones such as those by Victor Hugo, Proust and Colette, incunabula such as the Gutenberg Bible, first editions, old and current newspapers, along with almost fifteen million prints and photographs and over a million audiovisual documents. To solve space problems, the entire collection of printed matter was moved in 1995 to the four glass towers of the François Mitterand Library in the Tolbiac district.

At the far end of the Rue de Richelieu, there stands another temple, this one dedicated to finance, called "la Bourse" (Stock Exchange). Brongniard built it at the beginning of the 19th century, and it was enlarged a century later. Nowadays, transactions no longer take place in the famous pit amid the noisy calls of traders. Today, trading is done in a more sober, if not quiet, fashion via computer networks.

The quadriga of the Carrousel

Napoleon defeated the coalition fighting against him in 1806 at the battles of Ulm, Austerlitz and Jena. He had been King of Italy for over a year and had put Joseph Bonaparte on the throne of Naples, and made Louis king of the Netherlands. The Emperor decided to commemorate his victories with a monument that would leave his stamp on the Louvre, and chose the symbol of his ancient predecessors: a Triumphal Arch. It was built in the Carrousel Courtyard by Percier and La Fontaine, richly adorned with pink marble columns and bas-reliefs, and surmounted by a quadriga of gilded horses that had been taken from Italy during one of his campaigns. With the fall of the Empire, the horses were sent back to their place of origin and were replaced by copies, which gleam brightly after their recent restoration.

The Opera and the Grands Boulevards

The Opera

The Opera was inaugurated on January 5, 1875. It is known as the Palais Garnier, although the idea for this magnificent edifice came from Napoleon III. Garnier worked on the palace for fourteen years and perrsonally guided the Empress on a tour of the building which he called an example of "Napoleon III style." The statues along the façade were sculpted by Carpeaux.

Charles Garnier's opera house project was selected in 1860 from among dozens of others. Until then, the Opera had been housed in a number of different halls, forced to move from one to another by random events including several fires. Opera performances held a special place among social events during the Second Empire, and Napoleon decided to build a monument for the artists that would also be worthy of the elegant audience they attracted.

The cornerstone was laid in 1862, although initially, the builders had to pump out the groundwater that remained from the former course of the Seine. Construction work was interrupted by the defeat of Napoleon III and the Commune. President Mac-Mahon finally inaugurated the Opera on January 5, 1875, in the presence of King Alphonse XII of Spain, the mayor of London and the burgermeister of Amsterdam. It is the largest opera house in the world, with a total area of over 40,000 square feet. It has a seating capacity of 2,000 and 334 dressing rooms for performers.

In 1974, the costume workshop produced over 2,400 costumes. There were 160 dancers and 20 principal dancers, led by famous names in ballet such as Rudolf Nureyev and Patrick Dupond. The orchestra was composed of 146 musicians and a choir of 400 singers. Since then, the national ballet school, whose *petits rats* (the nickname for young dancers) once inspired the work of Degas, was transferred to Nanterre.

Some architects have taken the building as a model for opera house construction in other parts of the world, while others consider it too pompous. The monument nevertheless remains characteristic of the Second Empire. The arcades are surmounted by a loggia with double columns made from red Bavarian stone. Carpeaux sculpted *La Danse* to the right of the flight of ten steps. The original of this 19th century masterpiece is now at the Louvre, protected from pollution; the copy on display was sculpted by Paul Belmondo.

Garnier designed the magnificent grand staircase so that the Parisian smart set could provide their own show for themselves. The marble steps and columns are combined with onyx balustrades. Caryatids of *Comedy* and *Tragedy* decorate the entrance to the orchestra and the amphitheatre. The hall holds five floors of boxes overlooking an Italian-style stage.

The original ceiling was painted by Lenepveu. It was covered over in 1964 by a Chagall painting representing nine operas and ballets (Mozart's *The Magic Flute*, Tchaikovsky's *Swan Lake*, etc.).

In addition to the luxurious lobby, where many illustrious figures have strolled, the Palais Garnier holds another treasure: a library containing the scores of all the operas presented since Lully..

Surrounding the building is a monumental square situated at the intersection of a network of thoroughfares, some of which were built at the same time, including the

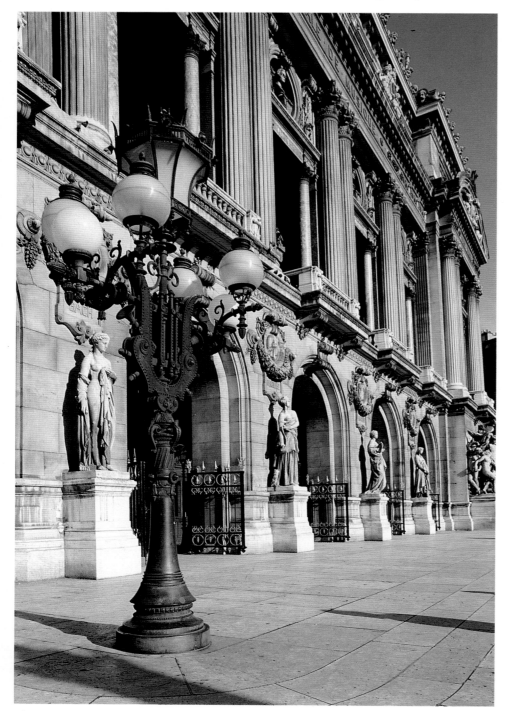

Avenue de l'Opéra, crossed by the ring of *grands boulevards.*

The large streets, first created when the city ramparts were demolished during the reign of Louis XIV, soon became a favorite Parisian promenade. In 1899, André Gide used the liveliest of the roads, "the boulevard from the Madeleine to the Opera" as the setting for his *Promethée mal enchaîné.* As soon as these large boulevards were opened, they became a hive of activity, particularly the northern ones running from Place de la Madeleine to Place de la République. In 1828, the first omnibus route travelled from Place de la Madeleine to Place de la Bastille. It reached the Boulevard Beaumarchais where the author of *The Marriage of Figaro* died in his *hôtel* at numbers 2-20.

The Boulevard du Temple was shortened and its buildings razed by Haussmann to make way for the Place de la République. During the 19th century, this road was known as the Boulevard du Crime, as many of its theatres presented melodramas about murders.

Among the most important venues, which have long since vanished, were the Théâtre des Funambules where the mime Debureau played the role of Pierrot between 1830 and 1846 and the Folies-Dramatiques where Frédérick Lemaître played the role of Robert Macaire in 1835. Only the Théâtre Déjazet remains standing today. It was used by the Comte d'Artois (Charles X). It became a small music hall called the Folies-Meyer in 1852 and was bought by the actress Virginie Déjazet in 1859. The Cirque d'Hiver, located in the Place Pasdeloup, is one of the only circus buildings left in Paris. Place de la République was built between 1854 and 1862, replacing and considerably enlarging the former Place du Château d'Eau. The Château d'Eau barracks were put up on the site of the diorama where Daguerre presented his transparent tableaux on glass in 1822.

The Renaissance and Porte-Saint-Martin Theatres, located on Boulevard Saint-Martin, where Lola Montès and Jeanne Detourbet performed in plays such as *Cyrano de Bergerac* and *Chantecler* by Edmond Rostand, are still in use today,. The Théâtre des Variétés on Boulevard Montmartre was inaugurated in 1807. The premiere of Offenbach's *La Belle Hélène* took place there on December 13, 1864.

The Grévin Museum is located at number 10 and has continued the tradition of Alfred Grévin, who founded it in 1882. The wax statues, which are

periodically updated, depict famous personalities such as politicians and film stars. The covered passageways in the area, including Passage Jouffroy, located near the entrance to the Grévin Museum, Passage Choiseul, Passage des Panoramas, etc., are interesting and worth exploring. The Passage des Panoramas dates from 1800 and its name refers to the large paintings on cylindrical canvas showing views of foreign landscapes.

The Opéra-Comique is also located in the vicinity of the Palais Garnier. It was inaugurated in 1783 to house the Comédiens Italiens theater company who gave the street its name, after they left the theater in Rue Mauconseil. In order to distinguish their hall from the myriad of small theatres around them, they decided to put the entrance at the rear of the building.

When the Bastille Opera House opened, the Palais Garnier became the "Palace of Dance."

Opéra-Comique

This theater is also known as the Salle Favart, in memory of one of the directors, C.S. Favart, often considered the creator of musical comedy, whereas Philidor is considered the creator of comic opera as a genre.

Place Vendôme and the Madeleine

Place Vendôme

At the death of the Duc de Vendôme, the son of Henry IV and Gabrielle d'Estrées, in 1670, Hardouin-Mansart and a group of financiers joined together to purchase the Duke's *hôtel particulier*. They ran into problems, however, and Mansart appealed to Louvois, the superintendent in charge of buildings, who proposed the construction of a square that would be both "very decorative" and "very convenient" for traffic. He wanted to outdo the Maréchal de la Feuillade at Place des Victoires.

In 1685, Louis XIV bought the Hôtel de Vendôme and the neighbouring Capuchin convent. Although the works started in 1686, they were not completed until 1720. H.-Mansart and Boffrand designed an octagon with two openings (north and south) and a triumphal arch. Girardon designed an equestrian statue depicting Louis XIV, which was unveiled in 1699 in the center of Place Louis-le-Grand.

The statue was destroyed by the revolutionaries who renamed the square Place des Piques. Bonaparte changed it to Place Vendôme and in 1810, he unveiled a column modeled on the style of Trajan's Column in Rome, recounting the 1805 military campaign and the victory at Austerlitz. Louis XVIII replaced it with a white flag, and later, Louis-Philippe put up a statue of Napoleon wearing his hat. Finally, in 1863, another statue of Napoleon, the one we see today, was placed atop the column by his nephew, Napoleon III.

On March 22, 1871, the National Guard opened fire on a demonstrators who were opposed to the Versailles government. On May 16, Courbet ordered the Commune to bring down the Vendôme Column as a symbol of "ideas related to war and conquest". When the Communards were defeated, Courbet had to pay the cost of having the statue put back in place. He sold his paintings and sought refuge in Switzerland in 1873, the same year the Third Republic re-erected it.

Place de la Madeleine

In the 13th century, a chapel in the town of Ville-L'Evêque was dedicated to Saint Madeleine. The building was rebuilt twice, once in the 14th and again in the 17th century. The development of the neighborhood and the creation of the Place Louis XV (now Place de la Concorde) suggest another aim: to build a monument worthy of the view of Rue Royal, the two *hôtels particuliers* by Gabriel and the Palais-Bourbon. The cornerstone was laid by Louis XV in 1764, and the works were supervised by Contant d'Ivry and then Couture. They came to a halt at the Revolution, and the old church was sold and demolished in 1798.

A number of project proposals were made during the empire of Napoleon, but no one knew what to do with the future building. Some favored a stock market, others the Banque de France or an opera house or a library. In 1806, the Emperor decided it would be a Temple of Glory, dedicated to his Great Army and inspired by similar temples in Athens. Vignon was put in charge of designing this imitation Greek temple.

Louis XVIII decided to transform the interior area into a church, and although no crosses were added to the building, Lemaire sculpted the large pediment depicting a scene from the Last Judgement, where Saint Madeleine is shown kneeling at the feet of Christ. When Vignon died, Huvé continued the works. There was further uncertainty about the building's purpose under Louis-Philippe, and in 1873 it was came close to being used as the departure station for the first railway line between Paris and Saint-Germain-en-Laye. The church was finally consecrated in 1842. From the top of the flight of 28 grand steps, one can contemplate a marvellous view of Rue Royale, the obelisk, Place de la Concorde, the Palais-Bourbon and the dome of Les Invalides. Triquetti sculpted the bronze door which measures 35 feet by 16 feet. The church has a single nave, covered and lit by three domes, and a semicircular choir. The hall displays the *Marriage of the Virgin* by Pradier (on the right) and the *Baptism of Christ* by Rude (on the left). The Durand restaurant is located in the square. It was used as meeting place by republican deputies in 1848 and by partisans of general Boulanger in 1889. Zola wrote *J'accuse* here in 1898.

Rue Royale and the Madeleine

Place Vendôme and Place de la Madeleine often symbolize the French capital, yet they have little in common. Both are very large but were built according to different plans, despite their similar geometry. Place Vendôme is decorated by a single column, whereas the church of the Madeleine takes up the whole square. Place Vendôme houses the luxurious window displays of the jewellery trade, whereas the area surrounding the Place de la Madeleine offers an upscale version of everyday life with shops displaying flowers, caviar, truffles as well as cheese, fruit and other desserts. In short, a luxury market.

From the Tuileries to Place de la Concorde

Rue de Rivoli and the Tuileries Gardens

Running from Place de la Concorde to Palais-Royal, the Rue de Rivoli is one of the most famous international areas of Paris. It houses two hotels renowned to foreigners: the enormous Intercontinental, virtually a city within the city, with its delightful inner courtyard. The other, Le Meurice, is favoured by a highly varied clientele. Dalí lived here for a long time, and it was the spot chosen by Florence Jay-Gould for her famous literary lunches. Napoleon had the Rue de Rivoli opened, entrusting the construction of the first part to Percier and Fontaine. It was extended to Saint-Paul in the Marais, between 1849 and 1856, and since then has crossed the city from east to west, parallel to the Seine. It was given the name of one of young Bonaparte's victories in Italy.

On the Tuileries side, the Museum of Decorative Arts is located at no. 107, where visitors can see a display of tapestries, earthenware objects, bronze, porcelain, jewellery and furniture, dating from the Middle Ages to the present. A toy museum and the Dubuffet bequest are nearby. The Museum of Fashion Arts (Marsan pavilion) also combines an historical collection with temporary exhibitions. At no. 230, a plaque recalls that the Salle du Manège stood here, which was used as a meeting place by the Constituent and Legislative Assemblies, and by the Convention in its early days. The First Republic was proclaimed here on September 21, 1792.

In 1564, Catherine de Medecis ordered the construction of a castle near the Louvre to accommodate her entourage. The building was erected some 500 yards away, on the site of two tile factories. Philibert Delorme and later Jean Bullant were put in charge of building the Tuileries palace. The Queen decided to join it to the Louvre by a long gallery along the Seine. Problems arose because the façades were not parallel, and the Louvre's east-west axis did not coincide with the Tuileries façade.

The Queen halted the works in 1572, after reading an unfavorable horoscope. Catherine, the niece of Pope Clement VII, had always attached great importance to astrologers, and even had the famous astrologer Ruggieri come all the way from Florence to advise her. She never lived at the Tuileries.

The construction of the Grand Gallery started again under Henry IV in 1595, and Jacques II Androuet du Cerceau built the Flore Pavilion at one end. The Tuileries palace was attached to the Louvre by means of a small gallery.

Louis XIV confided the construction of Marsan pavilion to Le Vau and ordered the remodelling of the area. He only lived there for three years, however, and Louis XV for six. During the periods when it was abandoned by the royal family, the palace was occupied by noblemen, craftsmen and artists.

On October 6, 1789, the revolutionary mob forced Louis XVI and his family to abandon Versailles and move into the Tuileries. When the palace was stormed on August 10, 1792, Louis XVI had to take refuge in the Salle du Manège beside the deputies of the Legislative Assembly. When the Republic was proclaimed, the Tuileries became the headquarters of the Convention.

Napoleon I, Louis XVIII and Charles X all lived here. The palace was invaded during the revolution in 1830 and Louis-Philippe moved in before he was captured by the revolutionaries in 1848, when the Tuileries palace was occupied again. Napoleon III was the castle's last resident, living there until the revolution in 1870.

During the fighting between the Versailles followers and the Communards, the palace was set on fire: the floors and roof collapsed and the interior decoration was seriously damaged. Nonetheless, the walls, façades and staircases were still standing. Finally, in 1882, the Chamber of Deputies voted to have it demolished.

In 1884 all that was left were the Marsan and Flore pavilions, located at ends of the Louvre wings. Both of them were reconstructed.

The only vestige of the domain of Catherine de Medicis is the large esplanade she had cleared along the Seine. In the 16th century, it was described as a "beautiful garden… containing not only mazes, groves, streams and

Rue de Rivoli

This very long street changes its appearance between the beginning and the end. It starts at Saint-Paul, by the Carnavalet Museum in the Marais, and ends at Place de la Concorde. The residential area, with identical houses built atop a series of arcades, is divided into two parts. From the Rue du Louvre to the Rue des Pyramides, it runs opposite the north façade of the Louvre. After the Place des Pyramides, there is nothing between the street and Seine but the the Tuileries Gardens.

fountains, but also reproductions of the seasons and the signs of the zodiac….”

The Italian-style garden was opened to the public and became a fashionable area for promenades. Le Nôtre transformed it into a French-style garden in 1664, extending it with a path towards the hill of Chaillot (the future Champs-Elysées), with two terraces that could be reached via two wide ramps and decorated with four

Impressionist collection was transferred to the Orsay Museum from the Jeu de Paume, which is now a venue for temporary exhibitions. The Orangerie Museum displays a number of huge canvases of waterlilies painted by Monet at his house in Giverny, along with the Walter-Guillaume private collection, including Cézanne, Renoir (*Girls at the Piano*), Soutine, Picasso (*The Embrace*), le Douanier Rousseau (*La carriole du Père Junier*), Derain,

ornamental ponds. The public's infatuation with the gardens contributed to the city's westward expansion.

In 1783, Charles and Robert's gas balloon made one of its first ascensions here. Robespierre celebrated his Feast of the Supreme Being here on June 8, 1794: the semicircle of marble benches at the beginning of the central pathway date from that event.

On the Place de la Concorde side, there are many statues such as *Les Renommées* and Mercury on winged horses by Coysevox, a bust of Le Nôtre by the same sculptor, and *La femme couchée* by Maillol. The

Utrillo, Matisse, Modigliani (*The Young Apprentice*).

On the Louvre side, there is a large series of dynamic, voluptuous statues created by Aristide Maillol in 1964 thanks to a generous donation by Dina Vierny, his principal model. The Place du Carrousel is named after the equestrian show put on by Louis XIV to celebrate the birth of the first Dauphin. The elegant Triumphal Arch with its pink marble Corinthian columns commemorates Napoleon's victories in 1805. It was built by Percier and Fontaine between 1806 and 1808, imitating the arch of Septimius Severus in Rome.

Place de la Concorde

Ramses, one day my splendid block,
On which eternity cracked and split,
Rolled here, mown down like a blade of grass,
And Paris made a plaything of it.
Théophile Gautier

more than 275,000 square feet, bordered by a ditch that Napoleon III had filled. The only remaining vestige today is a stone balustrade.

There are two mansions in the square presenting triangular pediments and Corinthian columns that create a composition reminiscent of Perrault's colonnade in the Louvre but with the lightness and elegance of Louis XV-style constructions. The building on the right was first

Place de la Concorde

This square was built in honor of Louis XV and originally bore his name. It was designed by Gabriel with rare elegance and was completed by Hittorf. It was first called Place de la Concorde in 1775, and recovered the name again in 1830.

The obelisk

The column is 75 feet tall, and has a twin brother in Luxor, Egypt.

In this poem, Gautier attributes nostalgic feelings to the obelisk that was moved to the center of the square in 1836 and later became its symbol.

The merchant's provost and the Parisian aldermen presented Louis XV with a statue of himself by Bouchardon, and a new royal square was built to receive it. Gabriel's project was chosen from among 18 other candidates. Beyond the Tuileries Gardens, there was nothing but muddy paths (now Rue Royale and the Champs-Elysées), trees and market gardens. The King granted the land to the City of Paris and Place Louis XV was completed in 1772. The octagonal area occupied

used as the royal furniture depositary and became the Ministry of the Navy after the royal family was forced to return to Paris in 1789. The other palace bears the name of the Duc de Crillon, and is located on the opposite side of the Rue Royale, with its luxury shops leading up to the Place de la Madeleine. The building was formerly divided into four apartments, and between 1805 and 1807 Chateaubriand lived in one of them. The United States Embassy is located on the other side of Rue Boissy-d'Anglas.

The old mansion of the Duc de la Vrillière, designed by Gabriel and constructed by Chalgrin, is located on the Tuileries side, on the corner of the rue Saint-Florentin. The Duke left fewer traces in history than Talleyrand, one of his successors in this building, who died here in 1838. Few diplomats enjoyed such a long life or adapted as easily as Talleyrand, who was a bishop (under the monarchy), became the leader of the constitutional clergy before emigrating when charged with treason during the Revolution, and later joined the Emperor. In 1814, he was in favor of the Restoration and at the end of his career, he became an ambassador of Louis-Philippe.

On May 30, 1770, a fireworks display was held in the square to celebrate the marriage of Louis, the dauphin, and Marie-Antoinette. A fire started up and over one hundred people were crushed by the crowd in the ensuing panic.

In 1792, the statue of Louis XV was melted down and the square was decorated with a Statue of Liberty. The bridge was completed in 1791, using stones from the demolition of the Bastille.

The square was known as Place de la Revolution where the guillotine was installed in 1772. Over a thousand people were beheaded here, including Louis XVI, Marie-Antoinette, Charlotte Corday, Brissot and the Girondins, Madame Roland, Hébert, Danton, Lavoisier, Robespierre, Saint-Just, etc. The last victims were the *sans-culotte* rebels of the 1st Prairial III (May 20, 1795).

The square was renamed Place de la Concorde during the Directoire, to establish the fact that both the Revolution and the monarchy were abolished. David ordered the *Marly Horses* by Guillaume Coustou to be placed at the entrance to the Champs-Elysées in 1794, opposite Coysevox's winged horses located at the entrance to the Tuileries. Louis-Philippe ordered eight statues representing French cities by Gabriel, which were placed on pedestals: Lille, Strasbourg, Lyon, Marseille (to the east), Bordeaux, Nantes, Brest and Rouen (to the west). Hittorf, who had decorated the Summer Circus on the Champs-Elysées, designed two basin fountains and candelabra. The problem of finding a suitable central monument was resolved when the viceroy of Egypt, Mehemet-Ali, presented the city with the Luxor obelisk. The ensuing revolutions never threatened this symbol of a foreign sovereign (Ramses II) who died thirteen centuries before the modern era. It was raised on October 25, 1836 by the engineer Lebas, who took all the necessary precautions to hoist the 200-ton monument.

The Champs-Elysées

The Petit Palais and the Grand Palais

The first World Fair in Paris opened on May 15, 1885, four years after the one in London. For some time, the architects of the capital had been engaged in vast works projects under the aegis of Haussmann. The city map now featured large, well laid-out avenues where small, insalubrious streets had been razed and cleared land was ready for new buildings.

The prestigious exhibition required the construction of specific buildings like the Palace of Industry (inaugurated for the occasion, though it did not survive for long). A project was soon adopted to build two palaces on the street that would become the Avenue Alexandre III, which had already been opened up at the cost of destroying the Palace of Industry.

The palaces were finally built for another fair, planned to open the 20th century. Today, along with the Gare Orsay (now the Impressionist museum), they are the only buildings left from the World's Fair of 1900, where millions of people visited the pavilions set up on the Invalides esplanade.

The Grand Palais was erected on the other side of the river; it was designed by Deglane, whose project included a central metal-framed hall covered by a stone "shirt". He was awarded first prize, but the probjects submitted by Thomas and Louvet were also well received. It was therefore decided that the three architects would join forces, with each one responsible for the construction of a specific part of the building.

Deglane built the façade facing Avenue Alexandre III. He designed long porticos made up of gigantic Ionic columns on either side of the monumental entrance, and placed Fournier's glass mosaics behind them. Each wing ends in a concave pavilion crowned with a chariot drawn by horses leaping into the air.

Thomas designed the façade giving onto what is now Aveunue Franklin Roosevelt. His approach was in keeping with that of Deglane and he entrusted the decoration to his students, who designed bas-reliefs that were made at the Manufacture de Sèvres. He also created a vestibule for his wing, in which typical 1900s motifs are found alongside classical motifs, clearly influenced by Versailles.

Louvet designed the staircase leading up to the first floor, easily demonstrating that in that transitional period, a classical architect could use contemporary motifs without demeaning himself. This was the origin of the "modern style."

The light coming through the large glass roof, made possible by the recent mastery of metal and steel, created an unexpectedly warm atmosphere inside the building.

The Grand Palais is currently used for a variety of activities. The south section is a residence for students from the Sorbonne; the west wing houses the Palais de la Découverte (an excellent science museum, with a marvellous Planetarium), the north wing is dedicated to enormously successful art exhibitions, such as those of Gaugin and Renoir; the halls opposite the Petit Palais are used for shows such as the book fair or the annual contemporary art show.

The Petit Palais was constructed on trapezoidal-shaped land and is separated from the Grand Palais by Avenue Winston Churchill which runs up to the Alexandre III bridge crossing over to the Invalides esplanade on the Left Bank. Charles Girault carried out a meticulous analysis of the land before designing his project.

The entrance facing the avenue was an extremely important part of the construction. The majestic portal surmounted by a large curved pediment is reminiscent of Libéral Bruant's work on the Hôtel des Invalides.

Girault had the vestibule covered by a dome and closed off the palace with a gate combining 18th century elements with the natural decor. He erected colonnades on either side of the façade, like those of Deglane at the Grand Palais, with a pavilion at each end. Owing to the sharp angle of the buildings, the façades on the Cours-la-Reine and the Champs-Elysées are curved. Each pavilion is crowned by a hull-shaped roof.

Girault designed a semicircular courtyard surrounded by colonnades, behind which Badouin painted a series of frescoes.

In fact, Girault drew abundantly on 17th and 18th century styles, but everywhere he made a show of wealth that seemed to be the prerogative of the triumphant Republic.

The Petit Palais has now been turned into a museum that displays the art collections of the City of Paris.

An aerial view of the lower Champs-Elysées

This view shows the advantages of architectural preservation, as no new construction breaks the unity of this elegant area. Nothing has changed between the Petit Palais and Place de la Concorde, the area looks just as it did in the late 19th century. There are noticeable differences between the Champs-Elysées before and after the Rond-Point. The Saint-Honoré quarter, parallel to the foot of the avenue, has not changed either; its 18th century mansions are still the same. One of the most famous is the Hôtel d'Evreux, which once belonged to Madame de Pompadour and is now the Elysée Palace, where the president of France resides.

The Champs-Elysées and Etoile

"We made our way towards the Champs-Elysées along streets decorated with light and crowded with people, where balconies float in front of houses like golden clouds, vaporous objects detached by sunlight."

Marcel Proust
(Swann's Way)

After completing the landscaping of the Tuileries Gardens in 1664, Le Nôtre took on the project for extending the path between fields and marshland, leading to the modern-day Rond-Point or roundabout of the Champs-Elysées.

It was called the Grand-Cours, planted with double line of elm trees, separate from the Cours-la-Reine created in 1616 by Marie de Medecis, which ran along the Seine from the Tuileries to the current Alma Bridge. During the 18th century, the avenue was given the name Champs-Elysées or "Elysian Fields", referring to the land where heroic and virtuous men went after their death in Greek mythology.

In 1710, the avenue reached the Etoile hill under the direction of the Duc d'Antin, who was in charge of the construction of the royal gardens.

In 1770, the Marquis de Marigny, Madame de Pompadour's brother and superintendent of the king's buildings, had the hill lowered 16 feet and continued the construction of the avenue up to the Pont de Neuilly. The avenue been the scene of many historical incidents.

On October 5, 1789, it was the site of the procession of women bringing the royal family from Versailles and the return from Varennes on June 25, 1791, then during the Directoire period, the *Incroyables* and *Merveilleuses* who made the Champs-Elysées fashionable by flaunting themselves there in extravagant outfits. Boatmen, merchants and acrobats came in increasing numbers. In 1814, the Cossacks of Czar Alexander I of Russia camped there with their tents spreading out to what is now Porte Maillot. Their horses caused a great deal of damage and they were said to be so voracious that they chewed the bark off the trees.

By the time the state transferred the property rights to the City of Paris, the Champs-Elysées was equipped with sidewalks and fountains. The areas of greenery, which were deserted in the evenings, became safer when gaslights were installed. Philippe Lebon, who invented the device, was murdered in 1804 while walking along the Champs-Elysées one evening.

The avenue was quite shady from Place de la Concorde to the Rond-Point and featured the English-style gardens mentioneded by Proust.

The luminous fountains at the Rond-Point, made of glass blocks, were installed in 1958. For along time, the headquarters of the weekly magazine, *Jours de France,* was located in the former residence of the Countess de Lehon, the mistress of the Duc de Morny during the Second Empire.

Avenue Matignon is filled with art galleries. It nd runs into the equally luxurious Rue du Faubourg Saint-Honoré which once led to the medieval village of Roule. The "faubourg" or outlying district began at the last Saint-Honoré gate (Rue Royale) and still has some of its beautiful 18th century mansions.

Patte decorated the Hôtel de Béthune-Charost (at no. 39, currently the Embassy of the United Kingdom). The Elysée Palace (1718) was originally built by the architect Molet for Louis-Henri de la Tour d'Auvergne, Comte d'Evreux. It was inhabited by Madame de Pompadour, later bought by Murat and Napoleon signed his second abdication there on June 22, 1815.

In 1848, the palace became the official residence of the president of the Second Republic, Louis-Napoleon Bonaparte, who later was proclaimed Napoleon III. He then moved to the Tuileries, and the palace was used to accommodate visiting sovereigns. It became the

Avenue Montaigne

What used to be the Allée des Veuves or the "widow's walk" is currently the star of the Golden Triangle. It is hard to imagine that two hundred and fifty years ago, the area was a huge marshland used for raising shellfish. It became the Allée des Veuves during the Revolution, featuring open-air cafés of ill repute. Everything changed with the Second Empire, and Napoleon ordered the construction of a Pompeian-style palace. The avenue has maintained its elegant look ever since, and the shop windows clearly rival those in the Saint-Honoré quarter, making Paris a mecca for international luxury goods shopping.

The Champs-Elysées became the center of elegance, and the route of choice for aristocrats on their way towards the nearby woods called the Bois de Boulogne. Café-concerts at the Alcazar in summer and the Ambassadeurs, circular "panorama" paintings and ice skaters from the Skating Palace (which later became the Renauld-Barrault Theater) were typical of this period. The only building left from the avenue's era of glory is the Hôtel de Païva, a pefect example of Second Empire pomp. It was built in 1860 and still has its décor and the onyx staircase that Gambetta and Sainte-Beuve, Théophile Gaultier and Goncourt, Taine and Renan climbed for countless receptions. Thérèse Lachman, a woman of Polish extraction, married the Marquis de Païva, the cousin of the Portuguese ambassador, and then became the companion of Bismark's cousin, which brought on an accusation of espionage and her eventual expulsion form Paris in 1877.

Today, the Champs-Elysées area is a business district and a prime location for the head offices of large companies as well as many boutiques and shopping arcades (Lido, Claridge, Point Show), outdoor cafes, cinemas, banks, restaurants, travel agencies and fast food restaurants.

Measuring 230 feet across, it is not the widest avenue in Paris, yet for many people it remains the most beautiful street in the world.

The Triumphal Arch is situated directly in line with the Place de la Concorde, halfway between the obelisk, Paris' most ancient monument, and the recently constructed Grande Arche of la Défense.

Not many Parisians refer to the square around the Arch as Place Charles-de-Gaulle, despite the official plaque placed upon it after his death in 1970. Most continue to refer to it as l'Etoile or "the Star", just as they refer to "Beaubourg" instead of the Georges-Pompidou Center. The square was already known as the "Etoile de Chaillot" in 1730, when it was the intersection of five large carriage routes. In 1770, the hill was lowered 16 feet and the square was given a circular form.

Its prestige was enshrined with the construction of the Triumphal Arch in 1806. In 1854, Napoleon III issued a decree ordering the construction of seven new avenues. The Avenue des Champs-Elysées and the Avenue de la Grande Armée replaced the old Neuilly route, and Avenues Wagram and Kléber replaced the Fermiers-Géneraux rampart walk.

The Païva Staircase

It is not hard to guess the mood of Girardin, Théophile Gautier, Sainte-Beuve (and many others) as they climbed the staircase of the most famous Parisian courtesan who received them in romantic splendor.

residence of the president of the Republic once again when Mac-Mahon made it his home in 1873.

Avenue Montaigne, located close by, was devoted more to pleasure than to luxury in the 19th century. One of the city's most famous ballrooms, the Mabille, was located there.

The ballroom featured stars such as Rigolboche or Queen Pomaré, who had an advantage over the Cancan dancers: here one could watch the show or join in on their pulsating polkas.

Financiers grew fond of the new thoroughfare under Louis-Philippe and later Napoleon III, and built themselves mansions and apartment buildings along it.

The longest avenue in the French capital is the famous Avenue Foch which was known as Avenue de l'Impératrice in 1854, and later Avenue du Bois de Boulogne or simply Avenue du Bois (forest). It received its current name in 1929.

It was designed as a triumphal road by Hittorf and Haussman, measuring 4,268 feet long and 393 feet wide. During the Second Empire, luxurious carriages paraded along the avenue, going to and from the Bois de Boulogne, and many private residences were built alongside it.

The seven other main avenues were inaugurated in 1857: Friedland, Reine Hortense (Hoche), Roi Jerôme (Mac-Mahon), Essling (Carnot), Eylau (Victor Hugo), Iéna and Josephine (Marceau). The star with twelve perfectly geometrical roads leading out from the center was surrounded by twelve symmetrical mansions which were only 52 feet high so as to enhance the height of the Triumphal Arch.

The Place de l'Etoile had a diameter of 787 feet and was traced inside the circle formed by Rue Presbourg and Rue Tilsitt. Baron Haussmann thought it would make it easier for traffic to circulate in the Place itself. None of the projects conceived under Louis XV came to fruition, and it was finally Napoleon who issued a decree on February 18, 1806, after his victory at Austerlitz, adopting Chalgrin's project for a Triumphal Arch to celebrate the vistories of the Empire.

The Triumphal Arch in the Place du Carrousel is only 47 feet high and 65 wide (a more beautiful and harmonious construction) and Constantine's Arch in Rome measures 82 feet by 68, whereas the Triumphal Arch at Place de l'Etoile is 164 feet high and 147 feet wide. Neither Napoleon nor Chalgrin ever saw the project completed.

When Empress Marie-Louise entered Paris in 1810, the Arch was only a wooden frame covered with painted canvas, as the actual building was hardly above the foundations (it had taken two years to secure them solidly).

In 1823, Louis XVIII decided to continue the works to further the Restoration. The masonry was not completed until the reign of Louis-Philippe in 1831. Rude sculpted the Departure of the Army of 1792 (otherwise known as *La Marseillaise*) while Etex carved the *Résistance of the French in 1814* and *The Peace of 1815* and Corto *The Triumph of 1810*.

The entablature was decorated with a frieze recalling the departure of the French army and their victorious return, depicting hundreds of men, all of them six feet five inches tall.

In 1836, the names of the generals and the battles won by the Empire were engraved on the stone. Some names were omitted, leading to protests, especially by Victor Hugo whose father, General Joseph Hugo, had been left out.

Four years later, in December 1840, Napoleon's ashes were brought back to France and the procession passed under the Arch, drawing crowds of spectators. The Emperor's mortal remains had been repatriated from

The Cock Gate

The superb French emblem crowns the discreet exit from the Elysées Palace (on to the sober, elegant Avenue Gabriel). In 1969, when journalists were waiting for General De Gaulle on the Rue Saint-Honoré, he had left the palace by this gate after proposing his referendum.

The Champs-Elysées

For a long time, the Triumphal Arch which closes the triumphal route of the Avenue des Champs-Elysées, marked the end of the western view of Paris. Today, the Grand Arch at La Défense which can be seen in the distance, relegates Napoleon's arch to just another traditional monument. The Grand Arch silhouette appears to be an opening to the Paris of the 21ˢᵗ century, and the enlargement of La Défense quarter was considered a logical result. The steel, the glass and the Grand Arch itself, situated on the axis starting at the Carrousel (some say it begins at Notre-Dame) are all major aesthetic attractions, which leave the lively part of the Champs-Elysées in an awkward position. On the Carrousel side of the intersection lies is a timeless area of greenery; beyond the Triumphal Arch there is a different yet equally timeless architecture; in the center, "Les Champs", with its shop signs and neon lights. The prestigious avenue recovers its harmonious look every year for a few weeks when the it is decorated with Christmas lights.

Saint Helena; they travelled up along the Seine to Courbevoie and were taken down the snow-covered Champs-Elysées to Les Invalides.

In June 1885, Victor Hugo was honored here with a national funeral. Streetlampss were draped in crepe, flags flew at half-mast and a black cloth partially hid the monument around Gabriel's 75-foot-high catafalque. The tomb of the unknown soldier was placed here in 1921 and an eternal flame has been burning next to it since 1923.

Every year the Champs-Elysées appear in full regalia for Bastille Day on July 14.

The French Army displays its latest acquisitions; the various military corps parade from l'Etoile (Place Charles de Gaulle) to Place de la Concorde to salute the President of the Republic and his guests. As Haussmann once said: "This beautiful layout, which I am proud of having designed… can be viewed as a whole from the top of the Triumphal Arch, which is climbed by more foreigners than Parisians."

The 16th Arrondissement

For some, the 16th arrondissement correponds to a microcosm of frivolous, vain pursuits, synonymous with rather showy opulence, while for others it symbolizes success. This arrondissement never fails to arouse a reaction, though those who do not know it well have trouble imagining its diversity.

Each arrondissement has its good and bad neighborhoods, but here the city authorities stigmatized the price per square foot by dividing the 16th into two parts, north and south, with two different postal codes: 75116 and 75016. At the present time, the southern boundaries of the 16th, which a few years ago "snubbed" Boulogne, are now completely detached from those of the northern 16th and Boulogne residents now look mockingly at some of the inhabitants of 75016. This heavily residential quarter of Paris is of quite recent creation (January 1, 1860). It used to be made up of a series of villages, and the injurious interpretation of 75116 and 75016 began with Auteuil, the first "village" bordering the capital.

Auteuil has some of the most charming "villas" in Paris, and is one of the best preserved areas in the capital. It often has a village atmosphere, and some of the houses look more like country houses for Proust's *jeune filles en fleurs* than private mansions.

The city limits of Paris have not extended out this far for long. Parisians used to come here to escape the congestion of the city. Around 1667, Molière stayed in his country house and Boileau was often his guest. The latter was so enchanted by the area that he decided to move there in 1685 and invited many acquaintances, most importantly Racine's family. Upon returning from Africa, André Gide built himself a large villa in the area.

The long Rue La Fontaine recalls how important water was for the 16th: its name refers to the spring that watered the village (but it owes its capital "L" to the writer of the famous "Fables" who often visited Molière). The arrondissement has preserved its springs, and in the northern section, enthusiasts come to Lamartine Square to fetch water every day.

Leaving Auteuil, one goes up to Passy, whose iron-rich spring waters are far more renowned than those of Auteuil. At the beginning of the 17th century, Passy made its fortune exploiting them. The village had more than just water, however; there were also vines that produced a wine very much appreciated by Louis XIV. The names of the streets, "des Eaux", "de la Source", "des Vignes" and "Vineuse" recall the country origins of both communities. There were also rabbits, and the inhabitants of Passy were allowed to enclose their fields behind walls to protect their gardens from the rodents.

Balzac was the quarter's most famous inhabitant. He sought refuge here when fleeing his creditors under the pseudonym Monsieur de Breugnol, which he took from his housekeeper Madame Breugniot. Between November 1840 and February 1847, he wrote *La Cousine Bette* and *Le Cousin Pons*, among others. His house at 47 rue Raynouard is now a museum, untouched by time.

Every village is known for its lively streets, bell tower and café. In Passy, the lively section corresponds to Rue de l'Annonciation, a pedestrian street that used to specialize in food and Rue de Passy with its many clothes shops; the bell-tower belongs to Notre-Dame-de-Grâce church; and in the 16th arrondissement, the "café" became a charming tearoom called "Coquelin". Located in the Place de Passy, it specialized in pastries and delicatery cakes that were especially prized by its faithful customers.

Rue de Passy ends in the Boulevard Delessert where the quarter changes abruptly: the road slopes sharply downwards towards the Trocadéro gardens.

Since 1850, many celebrities have been buried in the Passy cemetery whose tree-lined paths are located at the top of the Trocadéro. Long avenues that criss-cross the northern part of the 16th start from the place du Trocadéro, at the top of Chaillot hill.

The most famous one is Avenue Georges-Mandel which turns into Avenue Henri-Martin. This road, with a median strip lined with trees and luxurious apartment buildings hidden behind the gates of their private gardens, is an archetypal residential avenue without any shops. A warm note is added in autumn by chestnut leaves that fall in disorderly profusion from the mass of chestnut trees. The avenue presents typical examples of luxury rental buildings built between 1890 and 1914.

After their marriages, Anna de Noailles and her sister, Hélène de Chimay, lived here near the splendid Singer residence inhabited by the Princess de Polignac (née Singer). The Avenues Eylau, Raymond-Poincaré, Kléber and Président-Wilson all start from the same square, a mini-replica of Place de l'Etoile, located at the end of avenue Kléber.

Avenue Raymond-Poincaré leads to Victor Hugo Square and the long Avenue Victor Hugo (to the north), which is matched to the south by Avenue Mozart.

Avenue Victor Hugo is divided into three sections: between Place de l'Etoile and Victor Hugo Square, there are luxurious boutiques that give it an international feel; the area between the square and Rue de Longchamp is lively, a sort of micro-village with all sorts of shops, including food shops. After that point, it turns into a sober residential area, with luxurious boutiques without any ostentatious shop signs.

Next to Passy, another very sought-after quarter, La Muette and the Ranelagh gardens, end at Avenue Victor Hugo and Avenue Henri-Martin. It was so far from the city at the time of Charles IX, that he ordered Philibert Delorme to build him a hunting lodge there.

Queen Margot, the Duchess of Berry, Madame de Pompadour and many others, all came to the La Muette castle to get away from Paris or Versailles. In 1783, Pilâtre de Rozier used the park to send up the first hot-air balloon. The estate suffered under the Revolution, and was completely ruined when Auteuil's railway line was constructed. Henry Rothschild ordered the reconstruction of the La Muette castle in 1921.

All around the area, the residential streets that surround the Ranelagh gardens (named after an English lord who created the leisure establishments) are both similar and dissimilar to those in Auteuil. In Auteuil, there are "villas", whereas here there are paved streets lined with mansions built at the turn-of-the-century and luxurious buildings and rental properties. This type of construction can also been seen around Place d'Iéna, Avenue Foch and behind Avenue Bugeaud.

At the foot of Avenue Raphaël, one of these discreet mansions became famous: the owner, Paul Marmottan, bequeathed it to the Academie des Beaux Arts in 1934, and in 1971, Claude Monet's son donated sixty-five of his father's paintings which are displayed there.

Avenue Foch

When a prestigious access route was needed for the newly landscaped Bois de Boulogne, Haussmann exceeded all the hitherto adopted proportions. The Avenue de l'Impératrice was inaugurated in 1854, measuring 393 feet wide. Aristocrats appreciated the comforts of the new quarters, and noble families restored their reputation: in 1902, Boni de Castellane and his extremely wealthy wife, Anna Gould, inaugurated the magnificent Palais Rose modelled on the Grand Trianon. Their parties were the talk of the town in Paris, and the Avenue du Bois became a symbol. The Palais Rose no longer exists, but the avenue still still enjoys great prestige. The residents (most of whom are foreign) no longer make tongues wag.

The Bois de Boulogne and Bagatelle

The Folie d'Artois

When Charles X was still the Comte d'Artois, he loved wagers and parties. On a bet with his sister-in-law, Queen Marie-Antoinette, he ordered this "folly" to be built in two months. The Queen performed at the play held to inaugurate the "folly"; afterwards the parties held by the Comte d'Artois were more subdued. Though small, the residence was decorated in a highly refined style to make it suitable to receive the Count's guests. The inscription on the pediment, which is difficult to translate literally, means "small but suitable."

When Proust mentioned the "Bois" (Woods), he did not need to specify it was the Bois de Boulogne, as it could be no other: "It felt as though the Woods was not just a woods, it seemed to have a destination foreign to the life of the trees within it; the exaltation I felt was not caused only by admiring autumn…."

Before Boulogne became a synonym of elegance under the Regency, it was used as hunting grounds (as were many other fields around Paris), and was visited by sovereigns and lords as well as prowlers. The pocket of greenery is now bounded by the Seine and the ring of suburban constructions, but it used to be part of the large Rouvre Forest, which spread out over the entire western part of the capital, from Saint-Germain to Montmorency.

A village called Les Menus stood here until the 14th century. After that, some pilgrims returning from a journey to Boulogne-sur-Mer decided to call their church Notre-Dame-de-Boulogne and gradually the name spread to the hamlet and the neighbouring forest.

What is now known as "Porte Maillot" is a vestige of the walls erected around the forest in the 16th century to stop theives and criminals from meeting there. At the time, the estate was used exclusively for royal hunting, and had only eight gates, one of which was on this spot.

When the forest was restored and renovated by Colbert, Louis XIV opened it up to the public once again. It is well-known that the Sun King loved large, open spaces, gardens and order. Hence, he was interested in these woods located on the road to the Saint-Germain castle, near Versailles and decided to remodel them (exactly to scale) in accordance with the French-style garden, introducing straight roads and star-shaped crossroads, and a certain discipline in the horticultural domain.

Then came the fashion for "follies" (mad whims). La Muette castle became very popular with the Duchess de Berry and Louis XV and the Folie-Saint-James or the Bagatelle were built.

The park, famous for its magnificent rose garden and an amazing variety of flowers, was designed according to the English style fashionable at the time. It was named "Bagatelle" in reference to the small hunting lodge or "babiole" (trinket), that once stood there, which was bought from the Maréchal d'Estrées by the young Comte d'Artois. On a bet with his sister-in-law, Marie-Antoinette, he had a small white castle built in its place in two months. The architect, Bélanger, and the other eight-hundred men he mobilized to create his "folly", worked night and day to erect the building before the given deadline.

During the 18th century, there were already petitions demanding the protection of the Boulogne woods, signed by Fragonard and Vernet among others. The trees had suffered from several harsh winters and had been ravaged under the Revolution. The impoverished inhabitants did not hesitate to prune and even cut down trees for firewood.

After the Battle of Waterloo, Boulogne was subjected to other degradations: English and Russian soldiers set up their camps here and their horses caused serious damage to the surroundings.

Once again, Haussmann was called in to restore the area during the Second Empire. The Bois de Boulogne no longer belonged to the state; it was now owned by the City of Paris.

Alphand and Davioud carried out an astonishing metamorphosis, which elegant Parisians hastened to come and admire. The Bois de Boulogne became a spot for boating on newly-created lakes, listening to music in a kiosk, having tea in the open air or horse riding along the reafforested pathways.

Boulogne remains dedicated to horses, with two race courses: Auteuil and Longchamp.

The Acclimatation Garden used to be full of exotic animals and plants, but today it is an amusement area for children. It is believed that the menagerie animals, including a couple of elephants, died during the famine in 1870.

A walk around the Bois de Boulogne reveals that it is a "garden" of many facets, including the Shakespeare Garden, the Pré Catelan, the Museum of Popular Arts and Traditions and the Auteuil greenhouses. Visitors should make a stop at the beautiful Albert Kahn Gardens.

The Orangerie

This orangery dates back to the time when the English owned the Bagatelle. It was removed from the Crown possessions in 1832 and Lord Seymour bought the building in 1835. Until his death in 1870, he continued to embellish the estate which he had succeeded in extending, through good relations with Napoleon III, from 25 to 60 acres. His heir, Sir Richard Wallace, pursued the work along the same lines.

The Monceau plain

Naumachie

Like other 18th century aristocrats, the Duke de Chartres wanted an English-style garden. He entrusted the task to Carmontelle, who dotted the lawns along a winding river with little Chinese pavilions, windmills, workshops and ruins, such as the colonnade surrounding this large pond, one of the last vestiges of the garden. The colonnade probably came from a chapel Catherine de Médecis had built for her husband in Saint-Dénis.

The gates of Monceau Park

These famous wrought-iron gates are so evocative that they have the power to conjure up the whole Monceau quarter. On the outside stand the magnificent apartment buildings on the Boulevard de Courcelles, and inside the gates, marvellous hôtels particuliers *with private gardens giving onto the park. One cannot refer to the quarter without thinking of Proust and the way he meticulously described the lifestyle of its inhabitants.*

The Monceau plain and its prolongation, the Batignolles, are Haussmannian creations. The quarters were integrated into the capital during his "reign", in the middle of the 19th century. Until then, Monceau and Batignolles were two separate villages on the northern city limits.

Monceau was an old town belonging to the Abbey of Saint-Denis whose lands were a game reserve for great lords and remained sparsely populated until the the Revolution.

In 1830, both villages were brought together under the name Batignolles-Monceau, and were annexed to Paris in 1860. Batignolles was inhabited by the lower middle class (Verlaine lived there in his youth) while the Monceau plain achieved a residential atmosphere that the park's surroundings have never lost.

Nothing has changed much since Haussmann decided to make this new quarter the most popular residential area in Paris. Rental buildings and private mansions have resisted the passage of time, and today there are only a few new buildings in the quarter.

Proust gave a wonderful description of a family apartment at no. 9 Boulevard Malesherbes: "... a beautiful, large building with apartments as ample as the any wealthy bourgeois home during the 1890s. The impression that stayed with me, which I can still see if I close my eyes, is of a rather dark interior, packed with heavy furniture, closed in by curtains, suffocating under carpets, all of it red and black…"

On the other side of the park, Rue de Courcelles, he often visited Princess Mathilde, whose soirées brought the imperial aristocracy together. When the author recounted evenings at the Guermantes, he was referring to her salon and that of the Greffulhe.

Whether they were large apartments or mansions, the interiors were very similar, and the parishioners of Saint-François-de-Salles and Saint-Augustin (who grew fewer as the 8th arrondissement became less populated) were also very homogenous.

A century later, the building façades and the mentality of residents seem to be immutable, so much so that any reference to the Monceau plain carries with it an implied suggestion of permanence.

The dignified austerity remained inviolate, except for charming residences that housed until only recently discreet *maisons closes,* indifferent to the laws passed to close them down.

Today, real-estate frenzy has spread through the 17th arrondissement far more than in the 16th, and many apartments in the area have been replaced by office buildings. Some streets, however, sheltered by prestigious avenues, have maintained a lively shopping district atmosphere.

The former village square is now Place Lévis, named after the last owners who lived there. The famous market in the Rue Lévis gives this quarter a rare touch of colour in a quarter where many of the avenues are proud to bear no shop signs.

The long streets created by Haussmann throughout the capital, lined with buildings that all looked alike, replaced more varied constructions often surrounded by gardens. Perhaps to offset the resulting austere appearance, he saw to it that Paris was dotted with public gardens and squares. Many of them already existed, but he remodeled them completely, with the help of Alphand, who was in charge of rearranging the promenades. Monceau Park is undoubtedly one of the most beautiful.

A century earlier, Louis-Philippe of Orleans had used part of his fortune to buy land that owners no longer wanted, to be developed into a large, landscaped area. The pre-Romantic fashion had changed the focus of people's interest.

Pleasure houses known as "follies" were readily built, where carefree parties were organized, but the gardens were looked after carefully. The classical French ornamental garden gave way to the English style.

Following Rousseau's recommendation to live close to nature to be able to contemplate "God at work," from the end of the 18th century a a great deal of effort was devoted to recreating "wilderness" areas in aristocratic districts, as skilfully designed as they were aritificial. A few idealized images live on in the collective memory, such as Marie-Antoinette surrounded by farmers and sheep in her hamlet at Versailles.

In *Elective Affinities*, Goethe described the pleasure aristocrats had taken in reproducing a sort of original world in miniature around their residences. In the same vein, Carmontelle designed a park for the

Duc de Chartres in 1778, with grass decorated by false ruins, rocks hollowed out with grottos, a river and waterfalls, a large pond and – the heigh of sophistication – a few graves.

Whether a carryover or a metamorphosis of the "Vanity" fashion in painting, it was considered good taste to remind strollers that all joy is fleeting.

In 1852, the state bought the "Folie-de-Chartres", and the City of Paris became its owner in 1870. Today, babysitters have replaced 19th century nannies.

Montmartre and Pigalle

Although Montmartre is renowned for its artists and cabarets, it was named either for a Roman god or a Catholic saint, depending on the interpretation. Romans had already built an altar to Mercury (god of travellers) on the hills above Paris, at a considerable distance from the center of Lutetia, on the main road leading north. According to this interpretation, the name comes from a deformation of *mons Mercurii*. Years later, Saint Denis, was beheaded here (where Rue Yvonne-le-tac stands today). The Saint is said to have picked up his head and kept walking until he reached the place on which Basilica of Saint Denis was later built. Hence, the area was called the *mont des martyrs*.

A Benedictine convent was installed here in 1134, around Saint-Pierre Church. By 1686, the buildings were in ruins and the convent "on top" was joined by a convent "below", built on the hillside. The square and Rue des Abbesses are named after the latter construction and the Boulevard Rochechouart, Rue de la Rochefoucauld and Rue de La Tour-d'Auvergne after three Mothers Superiors.

In 1794, the convent was sold as national property and destroyed. Rue d'Orsel bears the name of a property developer during the period who gave women's names to the neighbouring streets: Rue Gabrielle, Rue Berthe and Rue Antoinette (which has since become Yvonne-Le-Tac).

Ignatius de Loyola and six companions founded the Jesuit order in 1534 in the martyr's crypt of Saint Denis, where he is said to have suffered his beheading.

The Jehan-Rictus garden takes up part of the area where the town hall of Montmartre stood between 1837 and 1860 until it was annexed by the City of Paris and became the town hall of the 18th arrondissement from 1860 to 1892. Verlaine was married there in 1870 and Clemenceau was elected mayor in the same year. Jean-Baptiste Clément took over during the Commune but Clemenceau returned to the post afterwards. Guimard built the glass roofs and the Art Nouveau lamp-posts that decorate the Abbesses metro station.

Rue Ravignan was laid out on a road that starting in the 14th century was used for the carts of winegrowers and the plasterers who extracted the famous "plaster of

Paris" from the gypsum in the hills. The poet Max Jacob lived at number 7.

Place Emile-Goudeau is named after a poet and singer from Montmartre who was born in 1849 and founded the "hydropathes" club.

The Abbesses of Montmartre grew fruit trees on the land until it was expropriated. During the Empire period, a small restaurant known as the "Poirier Sans Pareil" attracted many visitors by offering a meal served on a table under the boughs of a large pear tree. The restaurant had to be closed in 1830, when the widening of the plaster quarries produced a landslide.

In 1880, a hotel, built mainly of wood, took over the restaurant. The artists who lodged there nicknamed it "Bateau-Lavoir" (boat-washhouse), as its corridors were reminiscent of the passageways in a boat; the second part of the name is an ironic reference to its single water tap. Renoir lived there in 1885 when Suzanne Valadon was his model. Max Jacob and Van Dongen stayed in 1902, and Picasso, Apollinaire and Salmon in 1903. It is said cubism was born in this place. Braque, Derain, Vlaminck, Modigliani and Dufy among others were the next inhabitants. The residence was located at no. 13, but was destroyed by a fire in 1970 and rebuilt as an artists' residence.

Place Jean-Baptiste Clément evokes the name of the mayor of Montmartre during the Commune, who wrote the song called *Le temps des cerises*.

Rue Poulbot evokes the name of the artist Francisque Poulbot (1879-1946) who was famous for his drawings of Parisian urchins wearing large caps and trousers held up by a single strap. Pictures of these *poulbots* are commonly found among tourist souvenirs.

Place du Calvaire is the smallest square in Paris. Here one can contemplate wonderful views over the city while enjoying peace and quiet away from the crowd at the Place du Tertre. The Montmartre Historial Museum presents scenes from the area's past in the form of wax figures.

Place du Tertre has existed since the 14th century. The trees were planted in 1635, and once a gallows stood here. A Freedom Tree, planted during the revolution in 1848, lasted until 1871.

Place du Tertre

Artists in the making and Poulbot imitators still paint under the watchful gaze of tourists on terraces around the Place du Tertre. Montmartre has always had an artistic tradition, although its days of glory were those of the Bateau-Lavoir. Whether they lived on the hill or elsewhere, many painters have reproduced the windmills, narrow streets and cabarets in their works, including Corot, Signac, Lautrec and, of course, Utrillo.

On March 18, 1871, the government wanted to seize the cannons that had been installed there by the National Guard. General Lecomte was in charge of the operation, and he ran into opposition from the people of Paris. The rebels managed to stop Lecomte. Clément Thomas, one of the generals who had been in charge of the repression in June 1848, was recognized; he was arrested and shot. Lecomte suffered the same fate. Thiers' government fled to Versailles, the revolution of the Commune of Paris began and lived on until May 29, 1871.

Now the Place du Tertre offers only hastily produced pictures, as tourists cluster round to watch artists draw charcoal portraits or cut profiles out of black paper. The cafés are always full of people, yet one need only go a short distance away to find the real atmosphere of the old Montmartre.

Saint-Pierre Church is located on what was probably the site of the Mercury temple. The Benedictine convent was destroyed and the façade dates from the 18th century façade, but there are some ancient vestiges inside: the vault spanning the choir and the three arched windows go back to the 12th century. Together with Saint-Martin-des-Champs, Saint-Pierre de Montmartre is the oldest church in Paris.

In 1873, the French parliament voted to build a basilica dedicated to the Sacred Heart as a symbol of contrition and hope after the defeat suffered in 1870-71. Abadie began the works in 1875, but they were not completed until 1919, as it was first necessary to drill 83 bore holes, which were then filled with masonry and linked by arches to secure the foundations.

The Romanesque-Byzantine style is of questionable taste, although everyone seems to have developed a fondness for the odd-shaped white "pastry" overlooking Paris from the atop its 272-foot-wide dome, and 308-foot bell-tower. After taking the funicular from Place Suzanne-Valadon, tourists and Parisians alike contemplate the wonderful view of the city from the basilica steps.

Rue Saint-Rustique is the oldest street in Montmartre, and has kept its ancient cobblestones and houses. Utrillo frequently painted the Rue Norvins, now full of souvenir shops, art galleries and restaurants that attract many tourists.

Rue Mont-Cenis was once a steep path leading to the Abbey of Saint-Denis which the monks took for

Sacré-Cœur

The inhabitants of Lutetia dedicated the highest hill in the city to the god of arts and trade, which became Mount Mercury, though some etymologists believe the name Montmartre comes from Mount Mars. However, the most widely accepted explanation is that the name comes from Mount of Martyrs, since Saint Denis was beheaded on the hill. Today, the basilica of Sacré-Cœur dominates the hill and has become its symbol. The project was designed by Paul Abadie, who had carried out the restoration of Saint-Pierre d'Angoulême and Saint-Front de Périgueux, from which he took inspiration for Sacré-Cœur. Not everyone was pleased with the Romanesque-Byzantine style, although the building has since become one of the city's most symbolic monuments with its huge dimensions (328 feet long, 164 feet wide and 272 feet high, including the dome) and its dazzling white stone walls.

their processions. Berlioz lived at no. 22. Erik Satie lived at no. 6, Rue Cortor, and no. 12 of the same road is now occupied by the Museum of Old Montmartre. The museum is located in the oldest house on the hill, which was built in the 17th century and has kept its garden. Renoir, Suzanne Valadon and her son Utrillo all lived there.

The Montmartre vineyard still has over 3,000 vine plants in rows along the Rue des Saules. A festival is held during the grape harvest and bottles are auctioned off for the benefit of Old Montmartre. no. 4 is occupied

by the "Lapin-Agile" where singers maintain the tradition of Aristide Bruant's cabaret which was frequented by many artists who lived on the hill in 1903.

There are only two windmills left in Montmartre, although there used to be over thirty. The Radet windmill is at no. 81 Rue Lepic and the famous Galette windmill (painted by Renoir) is at no. 79. Van Gogh lived at no. 54.

After crossing Rue Xavier-de-Maistre, Rue Lepic turns into a lively market. It leads to Place Blanche, where the old Blanche Gate of the Fermiers-Généraux wall still stands, named after the white tracks left by the carts carrying flour and plaster as they passed through the city toll gate. The Moulin Rouge evokes the famous cancan dancers and the paintings of Toulouse-Lautrec.

At the foot of the hill, Place Pigalle is named after one of the sculptors of Louis XIV who lived on the street of the same name. Verlaine, Manet, Degas, Zola, Maupassant and Toulouse-Lautrec, among others, all frequented the Nouvelles-Athènes café.

Not far away, Mallarmé and later Henry Miller used to wander around Place Clichy.

Belleville and Ménilmontant

As there are no famous monuments or churches in Belleville, there are fewer tourists than in Montmartre, even though they share a similar geography and history. In the steep streets, between the Saint-Martin Canal, the Buttes-Chaumont and Place des Fêtes, one encounters a lively quarter where few houses have been replaced by offices.

Like the neighboring hill of Monmartre, Belleville has a rebellious, rural, artistic and working-class past. Perhaps the fact of being located in the heights of Paris encourages a certain degree of independence. According to tradition, Belleville is famous for open-air cafés and festivities as well as for protests. The last battles of the Commune were fought here, and the greatest name on the hill is still that of Gambetta. After defending the "Belleville programme," advocating freedom and liberty and the reduction of "social antagonisms," the radical deputy managed to flee from Paris by balloon to organize the resistance against the Prussians in Tours. The village of Belleville has only been part of Paris since 1860.

Many of its steep streets still bear water-related names such as Rue des Rigoles, Rue des Cascades and Rue de la Mare, reminders that the the hill's flanks were once covered with streams. Belleville's aqueduct supplied water to part of Paris for many years. Belleville is also similar to Montmartre in that its slopes used to be covered with vineyards and cabarets which were renowned in the 18th century, when the area was still located on the outskirts of the city.

Some of them attracted crowds of Parisians, often of modest means, although the occasional gentleman could be seen there, enjoying the wine made by the well-known Ramponeau, who has a street bearing his name.

Belleville was the site of one of the few theatres operating outside of Paris during the Restoration.

The open-air café tradition was perpetuated by popular cafés where artists, craftsmen and workers living on the hill gathered. Many of them worked in the plaster quarries, which were intensively exploited both to build the city of Paris and for export to the United States.

Saint-Martin canal

Despite the many locks and tree-lined quays in the center of Paris, the Saint-Martin Canal remained relatively unknown until Louis Jouvet and Arletty had a memorable quarrel on one of the canal footbridges in Marcel Carné's Hôtel du Nord. The film was shot in a studio, not in the hotel in the photo.

Rue du Télégraphe was named in honor of Chappe, who chose the spot to install the invention that would revolutionize communications in 1792. The curious device nearly cost the inventor his life, as he was accused of plotting against the Republic.

To reach the heights of Belleville, one passes through Ménilmontant (which means "half-way up"), a quarter with its own legendary past. There were still many "paths through the vines and prairies" when Rousseau used to walk on the hillside, and he described the place where he was knocked down by a dog while having a stroll. Two film stars, who later became symbols of the popular "Ménilmuche" quarter, were born in Ménilmontant: Maurice Chevalier and Édith Piaf, who has an entire museum dedicated to her.

The Saint Martin Canal runs along the foot of the hill, and has been an extension of the Ourcq Canal since 1822. The buildings along the canal were renovated during a major project to rehabilitate eastern Paris that began in the 1970s. However, time seems to have stood still for the Hôtel du Nord immortalized in Carné's film of the same name, and one can still picture Jouvet and Arletty talking about "atmosphere" on the footbridge below. The 1930s influence in Paris is most evident in the canal locks, which evoke another film about the poetic life on the canals called *L'Atalante*, with Michel Simon playing the bargeman. The Montfaucon gallows, located nearby on the Rue de la Grange-aux-Belles, was feared by criminals in the Middle Ages and inspired Villon's *Ballade of the Hanged Men*.

In the center of the quarter lies another special spot: les Buttes-Chaumont, a park designed, like all the gardens created by Haussmann, by Alphand. The English-style landscaping was done between 1864 and 1867. Alphand and Barillet took advantage of the hilly terrain to created a lake with a rocky peak rising 164 feet high, joined to shore by a brick bridge known as the the "suicide bridge" and an iron footbridge. In keeping with the fashion for picturesque elements, they crowned the gardens with a reproduction of the Sybilla Temple in Tivoli, near Rome.

Buttes-Chaumont Park

The small rotunda in Buttes-Chaumont Park is often considered the symbol of this huge space of greenery located in northern Paris. The temple, a typical of the 19th century the architectural fashion inspired by antiquity, dominates the adjoining quarters and offers an interesting view of these neighborhoods. Like the hill of Montmartre, the Butte-Chaumont is a reminder of the complex problems faced by the architects who were in charge of modernizing the capital.

Bercy

Since the 16th century, Bercy has been a port for wood and wines, and during the 17th century, beautiful mansions such as the Hôtel de Rapée and the Chateau de Bercy castle were built here.

The number of wine warehouses grew significantly starting in 1809 and cabarets were set up along the banks of the Seine. This bucolic setting gave way to the Palais Omnisports, a sports stadium inaugurated in 1983.

The construction was designed by three architects: Andrault, Parat and Guvan. It is a first-rate

There were two main reasons for deciding to move the Ministry officesto Bercy from the Richelieu wing of the Louvre where they had been located for the past century.

The first was that the Grand Louvre, another grandiose project, was to occupy the entire palace by 1993. The second was the fact that the buildings (which accommodated 5,000 government employees) urgently needed to be modernized.

Chemetov and Huidobro were in charge of the whole Bercy project starting in late 1982. The buildings

The Bercy Sports Palace

This sports complex, covered by a grass pyramid, houses a stadium for a wide range of indoor sports. The gradiose dimensions of the building can accommodate three times as many people as the Zenith and four times as many as the Palais des Congrés. Thus, events held here, such as the choirs of Aida, can assume quite extraordinary proportions,

location for all types of "indoor" international competitions.

This multifunctional, multipurpose hall can accommodate 7,000 persons and was intended for the performance of a wide range of sports: tennis, athletics, ice-skating, etc. Concerts also occasionally take place here.

The French Ministry of the Economy, Industry and Finance is another key element of the "Grands Travaux" (major construction works) policy, which began in the 1970s in the east of Paris.

near the Gare de Lyon were erected by two other architects: Arretche and Karasinsky. All five buildings taken together have created the largest office complex in Europe. Government employees were not in a hurry to leave the Louvre. The Minister of Finance was the last to abandon his gilded office for Bercy, where his new office, located on the top floor, offers a splendid panoramic view of the Seine.

A private boat shuttles the Minister to and from the center of Paris. A helicopter platform was built on the roof.

La Défense

Over approximately thirty years, the skyscrapers that were built in the western area of Paris ended up forming an entire quarter, which has become an international business center. The Champs-Elysées and its extension, the avenue that crosses through Neuilly, lead to the focal point of Parisian business activity called La Défense. The quarter was created in 1958, under the direction of Le Corbusier.

At the end of the 1950s, this section of the suburbs was rather poor and forlorn. The Nanterre shanty towns behind it were even more miserable and anachronistic. Hence, the renovation project encompassed a very large geographical area.

Given that nothing had been constructed here, architects were free to innovate and they built pastel blue apartment buildings with windows surrounded by clouds. They felt it was necessary to humanize housing in a suburb that had taken on such huge dimensions. Plans were made to build a new Manhattan between La Défense and Paris, which, like all innovative ideas, encountered a good deal of resistance.

Trade shows transferred from the Grand Palais and Porte de Versailles to the dome-shaped CNIT building became world-class events. Thirty years later, La Défense is apparently a stunning architectural success. The view of these intelligently harmonized skyscrapers, reflected in each other's gigantic bluish mirrored walls, are widely admired and rarely encounter sharp criticism today.

A paved, pedestrian esplanade nearly 4,000 feet long is flanked by about fifty large office buildings in an area that descends in tiers towards the Seine. More than seventy thousand people work in these buildings, in over four hundred companies.

The Fiat and Elf towers are the highest constructions (583 feet), followed by the Manhattan, Gan, Roussel-Hoechst buildings, and so on.

The CNIT was built by Zehrfuss, Camelot and Mailly in 1958. At first, it was used for trade shows, but now it now holds boutiques, a hotel, offices and auditoriums.

The Grand Arch is the most recent monumental construction on the east-west axis of Paris (Louvre-Concorde-Triumphal Arch). It was designed by the Danish architect Johan Otto von Spreckelsen, a teacher at the Royal Academy of Fine Arts in Copenhagen. His project was chosen in 1983, and consisted of a large, hollow cube measuring 360 feet high by 347 feet wide; the interior space is 230 feet wide (the same width as the Champs-Elysées) and 295 long, which means that Notre Dame's towers and spire could fit inside.

The building's 300,000-ton weight rests on twelve piles 98 feet high. It is oriented at a slight angle of 6.30° to allows spectators to see the cube as a three-dimensional object. It has the same east-west orientation as the Cour Carrée of the Louvre.

Many state-of-the-art techniques were used in building the new monument, which combines 4,000 glass panels and 35,000 plates of Carrara marble to achieve an effect of prestige and beauty.

The south wall houses the ministries in charge of Infrastructure, Housing, Transport and the Sea. The north wall and the lateral buildings house the offices of large companies.

An International Communications Hub was planned for the top of the building, but the idea was shelved in favor of an Arch of Fraternity built to celebrate the Bicentenary of the French Revolution. Visitors have a new panoramic view over the Paris region from the roof which forms a 2.5-acre platform.

Grand Arch

At the end of the esplanade, the Grand Arch is an extension of the road starting at the Louvre, extending through the Tuileries, up the Champs-Elysées and through the Triumphal Arch, each step an important stage in the development of Paris. The simple appearance of the cube hides the problems that arose during construction, which could only be solved by using the most advanced engineering techniques. The 300,000 tons of concrete are hidden behind glass and white marble.

La Villette

The Geode

This unique construction was designed by Fainsilber. The sphere is 118 feet in diameter, covered with polished steel in the form of 6,433 pefectly adjusted stainless-steel triangles that shimmer in the sunlight. Inside, a large cinema that offers its 370 spectators a gigantic image on the 3,200-square-foot semi-circular screen using the Omnimax process. The Geode is undoubtedly the most stunning element in the park, and reflects the other buildings on its mirrored-surface, surrounded by water.

The Villette is currently one of the most dynamic cultural areas in Paris, a lively area offering many scientific, artistic, educational and sports activities. Villette Park spreads out over 137 acres bordering the Ourcq and Saint-Denis canals.

The main buildings are the Zenith (1984), the Grande Halle (1985), the Geode (1985), the Cité des Sciences et de l'Industrie (1986), the Paris-Villette Theater (1986) and the Park (1987).

The Villette was once famous for its livestock market and slaughterhouses. The facilities were housed inside four large covered markets created between 1862 and 1867 at Haussmann's initiative.

In 1955, the municipal council of Paris decided to reconstruct and modernize the facilities.

The renovation project proved too costly and in its place, a national science museum was installed at the Villette in 1970. The slaughterhouses and the market closed in 1974.

Ten years later, in 1984, the Zenith became the Parisian palace of rock music; Philippe Chaix and Jean-Paul Morel designed the large concert hall to accommodate 6,400 people, named after the red "Zenith" airplane atop the concrete column, which is the only remaining element of the new slaughterhouse stables.

The Grande Halle used to be the beef market. It was built by Jules Mérindol in 1867, and was later restored by architects Bernard Reichen and Philippe Robert, who were the first to carry out a "conversion" project in Paris. The works began in the spring of 1983 and were completed by January 1985. The Grande Halle is now used for trade fairs, exhibitions, conferences and shows. It covers 5 acres and can accommodate 16,000 persons.

The Cité des Sciences et de l'Industrie was inaugurated on March 13, 1986, on the same day as Halley's comet passed over the Earth. It was built by

Adrien Fainsilber using the most advanced techniques available at the time. He transformed the old Villette slaughterhouse auction room into an interactive science museum which serves a variety of purposes, including leisure activities, communication, culture, research and teaching.

It is the largest scientific and technical center in the world, and also the most modern and fascinating. Fainsilber decided to keep the large slaughterhouse structure made of grey granite and blue metal, and surroundeded it with water in a moat system. He succeeded in creating a stunning combination of light, water, vegetation, steel and concrete.

Inside, Explora offers over 98,000 square feet of exhibition space. The adventure of technology, science and industry is explained through four main themes (the Universe, Life, Industrial Society and Communication), with multimedia shows, interactive software and miniature models. The presentations incorporate audiovisual and computerized elements to encourage visitors to take an active part in their visit.

Conferences and symposiums from all over the world are held in the international conference center, equipped with ultra-modern facilities.

The science news hall is staffed by scientific journalists, and explains scientific inventions and their impact on everyday life.

The multimedia library, with its research center on the history of science and technology, is one of the largest in the world.

There is an inventorium divided into two play and discovery areas; one is designed for children between the ages of 3 and 6 and the other for children between the ages of 6 and 12. For many youngsters, the exhibits are their first contact with the world of science.

Using state-of-the-art equipment, the planetarium unveils the secrets of space, the galaxies and the planets to its 260 spectators.

The Louis-Lumière cinema offers a variety of films and videos on technical or scientific topics.

In the enormous Parc de la Villette, near the Porte de Pantin, the architect Christian Portzamparc designed a Cité de la Musique with a national conservatory, a concert hall, an instrument museum, an institute of music teaching, an organ hall and areas reserved for shops and craftsmen related to the world of music. The Park was designed by Bernard Tschumi.

The octroi at La Villette

The restoration of this octroi *or tollhouse was included in the plan for renovating La Villette quarter. Paris once had toll houses all around the city, to collect taxes on certain goods. The last one was abolished in 1948. Like many others, the one at La Villette was designed by the architect Claude-Nicolas Ledoux (1736-1806).*

111

LES INVALIDES

NOTRE-DAME

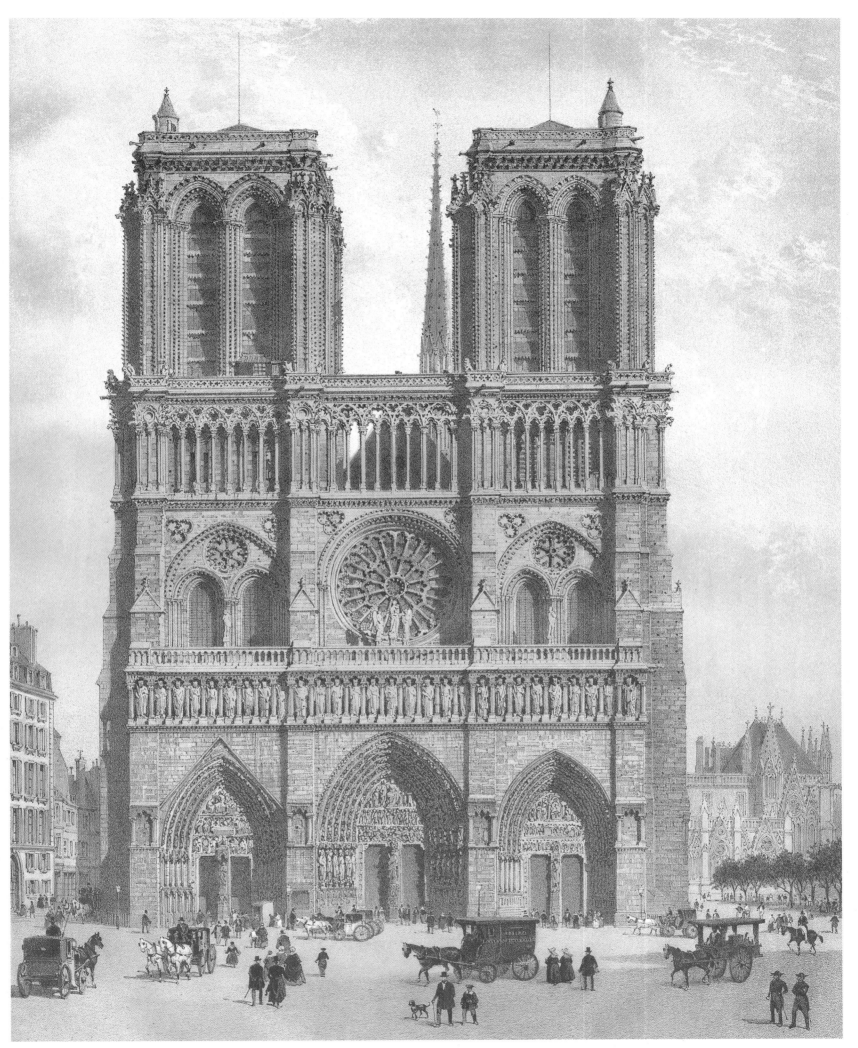

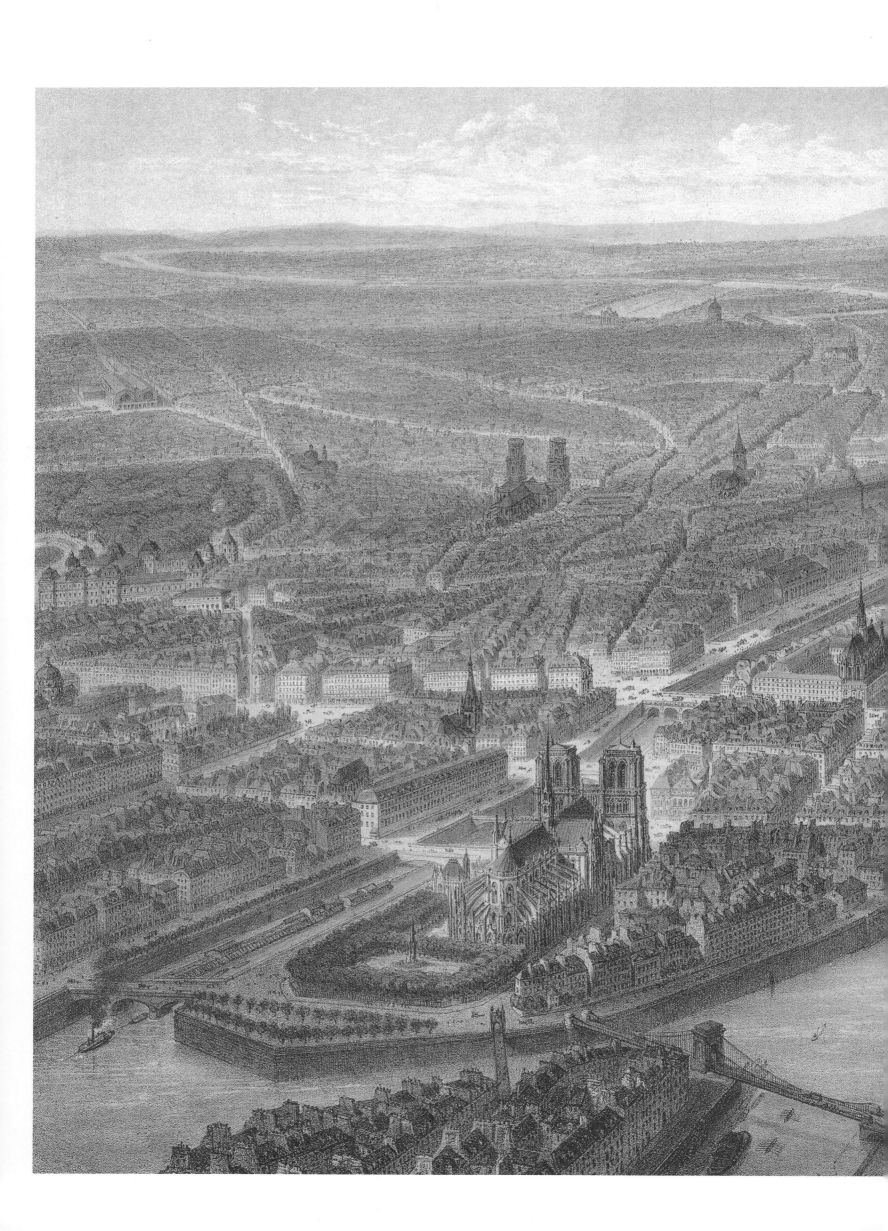

SAINTE-CHAPELLE

THE OPERA

GARE SAINT-LAZARE

NOTRE-DAME BEFORE 1772

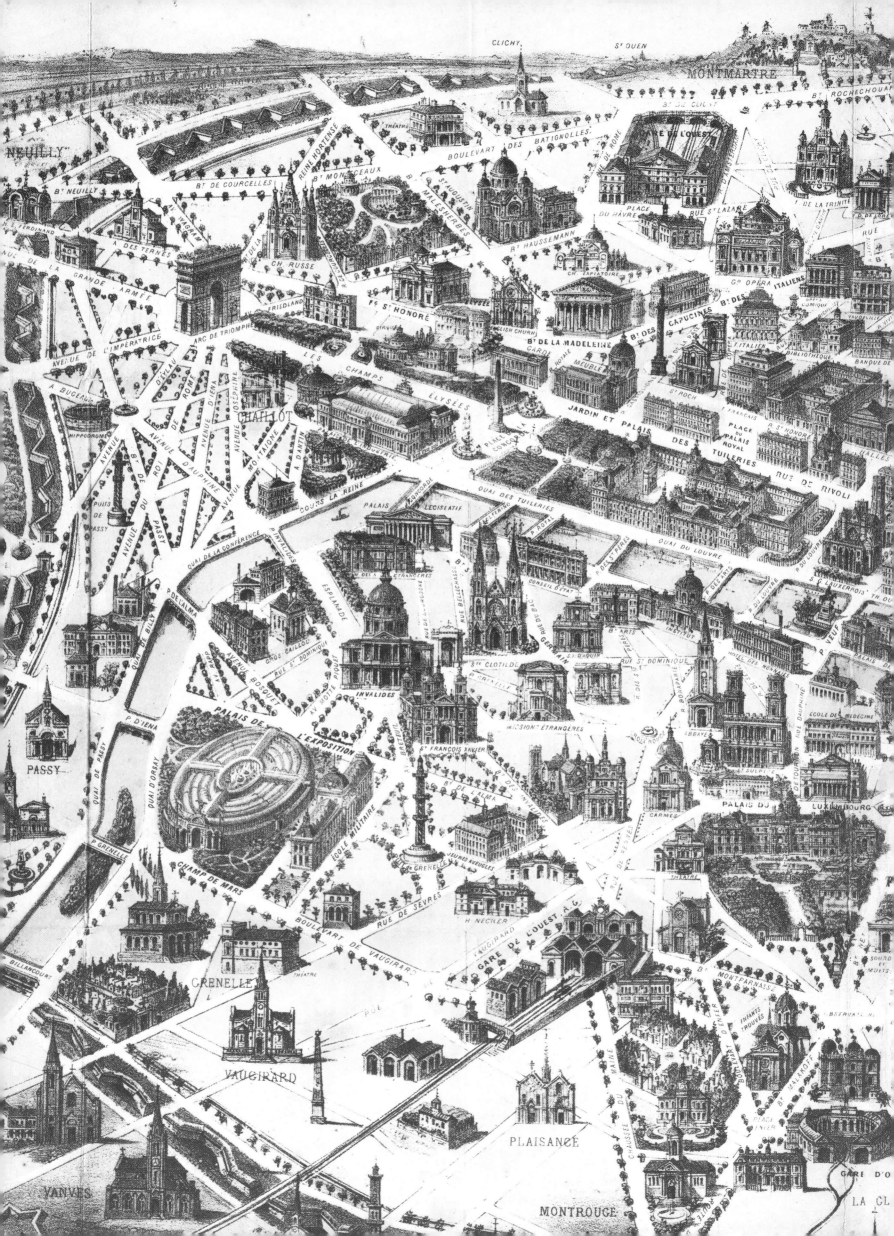